IS THAT DAMNED PAPER STILL COMING OUT?

IS THAT DAMNED PAPER STILL COMING OUT?

THE VERY BEST OF
THE DAILY WORKER/MORNING STAR 1930-2000

Edited by Mark Howe

PEOPLE'S PRESS PRINTING SOCIETY
LONDON

Is That Damned Paper Still Coming Out?

First published 2001
by People's Press Printing Society Ltd
Cape House
First Floor
787 Commercial Road
London E14 7HG

ISBN 0-9541473-0-8

Printed by Multiline Systems Ltd
22-24 Powell Road
London E5 8DJ
Tel: (020) 8985 3753

CONTENTS

7

Acknowledgements

Quotations from Claud Cockburn's memoirs and the excerpt 'My Days at the Daily Worker' appear with the permission of Andrew Cockburn.

The report 'Dogs Howl in Empty Almeria', under the byline Frank Pitcairn, appeared in *Cockburn In Spain: Despatches from the Spanish Civil War* edited by James Pettifer (London 1986).

'This Is a Sensational Article' by JBS Haldane, which originally appeared in the Daily Worker in 1939, was reprinted in the paper in 1964 with acknowledgements to Allen and Unwin; it has been published in a collection by Lawrence and Wishart and in *The Faber Book of Science* edited by John Carey (London 1995).

'Why Art To-day Follows Politics' by Virginia Woolf appears with the permission of The Society of Authors as the Literary Representative of the Estate of Virginia Woolf. The article was reprinted as 'The Artist and Politics' in *The Moment and Other Essays* (1947).

The reports and articles have been reproduced in full, with their original headings. Obvious literals in the paper of the day have been corrected.

Andy Vine designed the cover.

Nick Wright designed the typography and layout.

Sid Brown provided artwork and other material from the Daily Worker/Morning Star, including Ken Sprague's NHSOS cartoon.

Chris Birch, Miranda Gavin and John Haylett helped proof-read the book, while many comrades have provided advice and information about the paper and its history.

My thanks are due to all of these, to whom and to the paper's staff and loyal supporters over seven decades this book is dedicated.

Introduction

Mark Howe

"What! Is that damned paper still coming out?" The demise of the Morning Star, and its forerunner the Daily Worker, has, like the end of the class struggle or of history itself, been predicted often enough in the seven decades since the first efforts to strangle it at birth failed.

The detective who asked the question had been involved in the attempts to suppress the Daily Worker through the courts in the wake of the Invergordon mutiny of September 1931, when the paper supported the sailors of the Atlantic Fleet in their protest against the pay cuts imposed by the National government, with the Labour renegade Ramsay MacDonald at its helm.

The Daily Worker might have been founded to fight the National government – the regime of the Great Depression and appeasement of Hitler and Mussolini that led directly to the Second World War.

But the paper predated the National government by some 20 months and was itself "the fruit of a political fight within the ranks of the Communist Party, a long drawn-out conflict on whether the establishment of a Communist daily newspaper under British conditions was really possible," according to William Rust, the paper's first editor. "In the end the doubters and pessimists were routed," he added.

Rust's account of the paper's first two decades of struggle, *The Story of the Daily Worker*, published in 1949, remains the definitive record of the paper's growth, the struggle that went into it and the historic contribution it made to the fight against fascism.

The political fight to which Rust referred concerned, in immediate terms, what was known in the British Communist Party as the 'new line' – the third, or 'class against class,' period of the Communist International.

But this dovetailed with the determination of Communists like Rust to put into practice the longstanding advice of Lenin that the

British party must found a daily paper, no matter what.

As Rust quoted Lenin in *The Story of the Daily Worker*, "you must start this paper not as a business (as usually papers are started in capitalist countries) – not with a big sum of money, not in the ordinary and usual manner – but as an economic and political tool of the masses in their struggle."

Helpfully, the Russian revolutionary leader added the warning that the "English government will apply the shrewdest means in order to suppress every beginning of this kind."

But, as Rust recorded, a beginning of this kind was made when "on December 31, 1929, eight men gathered in an old warehouse in Tabernacle Street, London, EC2, in order to produce the first number of the Daily Worker, which had been promised for January 1, 1930."

Except that the eight were nine and not all men, including as they did one woman, Kay Beauchamp. The others were Rust, William Gallacher (the leader of Red Clydeside and later a Communist MP for 15 years), Walter Holmes, R Page Arnot, Frank Paterson, W G Shepherd, Brennan Ward and Tom Wintringham.

Thus, in a Quixotic act of voluntarism, when the Communist Party's organisation was still much weakened following the defeat of the General Strike in 1926, and when the party had embarked on a headlong course of confrontation with the rest of the left, was the Daily Worker born.

Yet the paper has endured for over seven decades – sustained alike by the same faith that gave it birth and those subtleties of the British labour movement that led Lenin to see its existence as essential to the fight for socialism in this country.

Over those seven decades the paper, which has survived far, far longer than any previous working-class newspaper in Britain, has created a uniquely sustained body of progressive and radical journalism – the embodiment of Marx's dictum that the point is not simply to interpret the world, but to fight to change it as well.

It is a tradition that includes reporters such as Claud Cockburn, Alan Winnington, Wilfred Burchett and Walter Holmes; the great cartoonist Gabriel; the legendary chief sub-editor Allen Hutt, whose training books set the benchmark for the industry; even the most successful racing tipster in Cayton.

This book is an anthology of the paper's living legacy, from the 1930s to the present. It is not intended to be a history of the Daily Worker and the Morning Star, but that history is recorded, subliminally, in these pages – as, indeed, is the history of the times through which the paper has fought.

That fight was joined in earnest less than a month into the Daily Worker's life, when "the shrewdest means" began to be applied to suppressing it, in the form a wholesalers' boycott which deprived the paper of a normal distribution network, at first in Lancashire and, by July, virtually throughout Britain. The boycott lasted for 12 years.

The response, driven by necessity, was to organise an alternative distribution network. As Rust recorded, "throughout the country our energetic supporters were to be found in the small hours of the morning collecting parcels at the railway stations and delivering them to newsagents or direct to readers."

By this unique means, "close, unbreakable ties were established between the paper and its readers, the selling of the Daily Worker became a regular task of the Communist Party and great public interest was aroused in the fight of a gallant little paper which was beset on all sides."

But the Daily Worker came under other, less oblique forms of attack – giving the lie to the myth of press freedom, which exists in Britain only on the terms of monopoly capitalism.

The paper was subjected to politically motivated libel suits, police raids and arrests, and on occasion direct police censorship of its contents. Staff were jailed, some even sentenced to penal servitude.

Ultimately, the Daily Worker was banned outright from January 1941 until September 1942 – not because of the paper's opposition to the conduct of the war, but because of the fear which its growing influence struck into the ruling class. The paper was not just an alternative voice, but was – and remains – a weapon in the struggle for power.

Certainly, the state continued to regard it as such, with threats made to prosecute the paper's journalists for treason – a hanging offence – for its coverage of the Korean War.

Even the most recent set of Cabinet papers released has shown that, in the early 1970s, the Tory Prime Minister Edward Heath made arrangements to have the offices of the Morning Star bugged as part of his war on the trade union movement, although it availed him not.

The defeat of the Heath government demonstrated, as have other episodes which flow through the paper's history like its very lifeblood, that elementary truth so hard to realise in practice – unity is strength.

The experiences of trying to forge unity in the struggle against fascism, both before and during the Second World War, gave rise to a subtle but fundamental change in the paper's basis.

Immediately after the war, ownership of the Daily Worker was transferred to a co-operative, the People's Press Printing Society, which owns and publishes the Morning Star – the name to which the Daily Worker was changed in 1966 – to this day.

The paper ceased to be the property and direct political organ of the Communist Party of Great Britain, although the closest links continued to exist between the two over many years, while the party remained an engine of class struggle.

The aim of the change was to strengthen left unity, to embody that slogan which appears on the masthead of the Morning Star today – "daily paper of the left."

· While the political toll exacted by the Cold War prevented that aim from being furthered in the ways envisaged by the architects of the change, the new co-operative structure embodied an important principle.

With ownership of shares open to individuals and organisations alike, but with voting rights accorded on the basis of 'one shareholder, one vote,' rather than the number of shares held, the Morning Star remains the only daily paper owned by its readers – the very antithesis of the monopoly capitalist press and broadcasting media.

The paper is, at present, a long way removed from the force it was when the People's Press Printing Society was established on the back of a wartime circulation of 100,000 copies daily and an estimated readership of half a million.

Partly, the paper's fortunes have fluctuated with those of the left as a whole, but bitter divisions have also taken their toll – over Hungary in 1956 and, more acutely, the rift with the Communist Party of Great Britain in the mid-1980s.

Now, after seven decades, the paper can at least claim equal rights with its critics to the benefit of hindsight – and examine what it actually said, rather than what the opponents of 'Stalinism' imagine the Daily Worker and Morning Star must have said.

The paper indeed supported the Soviet Union from its earliest days, as the strongest force for peace and socialism. But the Morning Star has criticised mistakes in the Soviet Union and other socialist countries over 35 years, while standing in solidarity with the socialist forces in those countries – and continues to do so.

But the paper's internationalism has always been far wider than any caricature of blind loyalty to the Soviet Union.

This book alone embraces struggles in Abyssinia, Spain, Malaya, Korea, South Africa, Vietnam, Cuba, Chile, El Salvador and Grenada.

There are many more examples in the paper's archives that cannot be reflected within the scope of this book.

But in the multi-polar world from which events can now be viewed, it can be said that the paper was right to side with the Soviet Union and, indeed, the world Communist movement against Maoism; was right to side with the Communists in Lebanon and Iraq against the phalangists and Ba'athists; was right to oppose the Gulf war and the war against Yugoslavia, to give but a few examples.

In Britain, the paper's stance for left unity and class politics was crucial in building the left advance in the late 1960s and early 1970s – the fruit of a long fight for left ideas and the struggle to break the right-wing grip on the labour movement, which remains as vital today as ever.

When the ruling-class counter-assault came, it was directed against the Morning Star, just as against the Communist Party and the broad left, but the paper stood foursquare with the miners during the 1984-5 strike and the printworkers at Wapping in 1986.

By then, a bitter struggle had broken out over the Morning Star, between the management committee of the paper and the leadership of the Communist Party of Great Britain – often referred to as 'Eurocommunists'.

The overwhelming majority of the paper's shareholders spoke then, as they have on other issues since, for the Morning Star continuing to exist as the daily voice of working people in struggle.

Through the strength of its ties with its readers, the Morning Star has survived and is now regaining lost ground – as indeed it must, as the only English-language socialist daily paper in the world today.

This book aims to reflect the best in the traditions of the Daily Worker and Morning Star – and the belief that those traditions are worth renewing.

As the Communist leader Harry Pollitt declared in January 1930, when the Daily Worker first seemed in mortal danger, "the paper is born and must never be allowed to die. If we keep that fixed in our minds we shall be invincible."

Workers of the World Unite!

DAILY WORKER

No. 1   **WEDNESDAY, JANUARY 1, 1930**   One Penny

WOOLLEN WORKERS TAKE THE FIELD

REVOLUTION IN INDIA GROWS

Congress Chiefs Feel Mass Pressure

The All-India National Congress, which opened at Lahore yesterday, adopted by 942 votes, against 798, the resolution moved by Gandhi, deploring the throwing of a bomb at the Viceroy and congratulating him on his escape. The minority, waving Red Flags, raised angry protests. Gandhi's second motion is to deal with the new manœuvre of withdrawal of "Dominion status" in favour of independence.

The reports of meetings of the Congress Committee in Session since Christmas Day, shows that the enormous rising tide of the Indian masses, led by the heroic Indian proletariat whose determined fight, marked by mass political strikes, is the enormous motive force which has compelled the leaders of the Indian bourgeoisie, who have in the past two years gone over to the side of British Imperialism, to make a desperate attempt to retain their hold on the masses by a show of opposition.

The resolution of the bourgeois nationalist leaders is in favour of independence and boycott of legislature significantly leaves the campaign for civil disobedience and non-payment of taxes to the discretion of the Congress Committee, "as and when necessary."

At the Sikh Conference meeting yesterday, also in Lahore, Khamb, Singh, the president, stated that out of thirty-one recent death sentences on revolutionary Indian nationalists, twenty-seven were Sikhs.

When Sir Frederick Sykes, Governor of Bengal, visited Ahmedabad two days ago he was met by a demonstration outside the station waving flags and with shouts of "Frederick Sykes, go back!"

SIXTY DEATHS IN CINEMA FIRE

Many Children Amongst The Victims

A fire which broke out at the Glen Cinema, Paisley, near Glasgow, during a children's matinée yesterday afternoon, caused a panic, resulting, it is feared, in about sixty deaths.

As soon as news of the fire spread frantic mothers ran to the Cinema, and began searching for their children.

One hundred and fifty people were taken to hospital.

It is certain that at least six children are dead.

FASCISTS WOUND WORKERS

Bauxite, Tuesday.—On Sunday night sixteen armed Fascists attacked a group of workers who were leaving a Party social in a thoroughly working-class quarter.

The Fascists fired on the unarmed workers and wounded four of them seriously. As usual, the police arrived too late —*Imprecorr*.

PRINCE'S JAUNT

To Travel Into Impenetrable Jungle—By Train

WITH HIS VALET!

On Friday the Prince of Wales will again start a jaunt that will cost thousands of pounds of the money the workers have earned for him.

He is going to Capetown, and from there will journey into the jungle—by train!

There he will display his intrepidity against the wild beasts of Africa. His valet is to accompany him, probably to hold the rifle.

An official of the "Kenilworth Castle," on which he is to travel, states that he is expected to play a prominent part in the "strenuous" deck games which are to be played on board.

"Otherwise, he will use an ordinary first-class cabin with the usual dressing-room."

SHOOTING THE UNEMPLOYED

Social Democrat Police Chief Orders Massacre in Cologne

Berlin, Tuesday.—Yesterday evening 10,000 unemployed workers demonstrated in front of the Cologne Town Hall in order to support the proposal of the Communist faction for winter assistance for the unemployed.

The social democratic Police President was in charge of large forces of police, who tried to prevent the demonstrators from reaching the Town Hall. At first the police used their batons, but when their efforts proved ineffective they gave the order to fire.

Many workers were wounded by the police bullets and over 100 arrested, including the Communist, W. Doerpinkgaus. The Communist proposals in the Town Council were rejected.—*Imprekorr*.

CLOSING THE RANKS

Woollen Workers Consolidate Against Wage Cuts

From Our Own Correspondent.

Shipley, Tuesday.—Rank and file conferences are to be called in the textile area to consolidate the workers' resistance to the threatened wage cuts.

To counter the proposed woollen wages' enquiry, the Bradford district committee of the Communist Party issued to-day a statement to all wool workers.

The statement compares the statement with the Lancashire arbitration, which served the same purpose of breaking the workers' resistance.

The woollen textile workers are advised not to return to work, but to extend the struggle, and to build up mill committees of action to fight against the strike-breaking court of enquiry proposed by the Labour Government.

MASS STRIKES AGAINST WAGE REDUCTIONS

Police Attack Pickets

ALL WORKERS SOLID AND DETERMINED TO WIN FIGHT

OVER two thousand woollen textile workers are on strike. The attempt to cut wages is meeting with real mass resistance. The workers are in a militant mood and maintain the utmost solidarity against employers, Labour Government, trade union bureaucrats and police.

The young workers are especially active and are giving increasing support to the Communist Party campaign for rank and file Committees of Action.

BONDFIELD, SCAB;

Labour Prepares to Smash Wool Strike

(From Our Own Correspondent.)

Bradford.—The council of the wool textile employers has not yet communicated on the letter of the Minister of Labour proposing to set up a court of enquiry into the situation in the woollen industry under Part 2 of the Industrial Courts Act, 1919.

Before availing themselves of the offer to impose the wage reductions by means of arbitration the woollen bosses are anxiously watching the strikes which are repeatedly breaking out and being carried on with remarkable determination.

I understand that Margaret Bondfield is going ahead with the setting up of the Court and that the constitution and terms of reference will be announced shortly.

DYE WORKERS STRIKE

Lightning Strike follows Dismissals

There was a lightning strike of 200 dye workers at the Kirk Lane Dye Works on Monday. The strike was due to the dismissal on the Saturday of 180 men.

Pickets were placed on the mill in the early morning and only the office staff and the key men on the mechanical side remained at work.

So far there is no news of a settlement and the works remain closed.

VOTE AGAINST WAGE CUTS

The strike at the Prospect Mills, Pudsey, continues. In answer to the opening of the mills in an attempt to impose a reduction of 1s. 6d. in the pound, a well-attended meeting of strikers held at the Trades Hall decided unanimously to resist any cut in wages for any section of the workers. A strike committee was elected and pickets appointed.

All operatives, union and non-union, are out.

DEFIANT SPIRIT

Determined to Resist Lower Wages

(From Our Own Correspondent.)

Saddleworth.—The attempt of the Saddleworth millowners to break the strike in nine mills against a wage cut of two shillings in the pound has completely failed. Although the mills were opened on Monday morning not one of the thirteen hundred strikers, mostly women and girls, returned.

The police have repeatedly attacked the pickets and some arrests have been made. The defiant attitude of Lily Hutton, a young woman worker, when "on trial" for assaulting a burly police inspector, typifies the spirit of the workers.

A long period of short time and low wages has made them determined to resist to the utmost.

Tom Thorburn, who was fined £10 or two months on a charge of assaulting the police at the mill gates, has now been released, the workers having collected sufficient money to pay his fine.

GREENFIELD STRIKE

Employers appeal to Labour Govt.

The operatives of the Kinders Mill, Greenfield, Yorks, are on strike and pickets are operating at the mills.

The employers' secretary has sent the following telegram to the Home Secretary:—

"Operatives of Messrs. Buckley and Co. (Greenfield), Ltd., Kinders Mill, Greenfield, Yorkshire, are being prevented by pickets from entering the mill, and are being otherwise intimidated at their homes. I am to ask that you will take such steps as will obviate intimidation of the workers and afford them adequate protection."

SCOTTISH "D.P.C." "DAILY WORKER" PRIZE DRAW. 1st: 15638; 2nd: 7056; 3rd: 5662; 4th: 7086; 5th: 15495; 6th: 2772.

17

'We are resolved to remain as one unit refusing to sail under the new rates of pay'

After a strike lasting several days the 12,000 sailors of the Atlantic Fleet have now weighed anchor, and the ships are sailing to Devonport, Chatham, Sheerness and Portsmouth. The Admiralty has been forced to promise an "investigation," but it is clear that a permanent success for the sailors depends on [CENSORED BY PRINTER] the action taken at Invergordon.

That the events at Invergordon were no flash in the pan is shown by the terms of the sailors' manifesto, which we publish below. A very serious movement is stirring the men in the Fleet and empty promises are not going to satisfy.

For the sailors now the big job is to stick to the demands set out in the manifesto and to obtain more and more support. Soldiers and

---

On August 24, 1931, the Labour government resigned and the Labour leader Ramsay MacDonald, along with several other prominent renegades, formed the National government with the Tories of Stanley Baldwin and the Liberals to ram through a savage programme of cuts. Unemployment benefit was to be cut by 10 per cent at a time of the highest jobless figures then ever known, over 2.7 million.

Resistance against the cuts reached its highest point with the mutiny at Invergordon against reduced rates of naval pay. The sequel of the mutiny is sketched in these reports, which provoked the wrath of the state against the Daily Worker. As well as the police raids described below, the nominal proprietors, Frank Paterson and Frank Priestley, were sentenced under the Incitement to Mutiny Act of 1797 to two years' imprisonment and three years' penal servitude respectively. In

airmen should realise that now is the chance for them also. From Belfast and other centres there come reports of messages of greetings to the sailors from mass meetings of the workers.

As usual, the sailors have set a fine example to all sections of the workers and Government employees. Are teachers going to allow their officials to "fight" the Government by inserting protest advertisements in the capitalist Press when the only way to fight is to do what the sailors are doing?

The blow against wages, pay, salaries and the dole may fall at any moment. The Orders in Council may be issued just when the Government pleases. The fight against the capitalist dictatorship and for bread and butter is on.

The sailors' manifesto

"We, the loyal subjects of His Majesty the King, do hereby present to My Lords Commissioners of the Admiralty our representative, to implore them to amend the drastic cuts in pay which have been inflicted on the lowest-paid men of the Lower Deck.

"It is evident to all concerned that this cut is the forerunner of tragedy, misery, and immorality amongst the families of the Lower Deck, and unless a guaranteed written agreement is received from

---

addition, one of the paper's sub-editors, W G Shepherd, was entrapped and charged with attempting to distribute subversive leaflets to sailors, resulting in a sentence of 20 months' hard labour.

William Rust, who wrote the note on police censorship reproduced below was the first editor of the Daily Worker, although throughout the paper's first decade the identity of the editor was not revealed publicly because of the threat of prosecution. The editor's chair was occupied variously by Jimmy Shields, Idris Cox, R Palme Dutt, Dave Springhall and John Ross Campbell, before Rust returned shortly after the outbreak of the Second World War, remaining the paper's editor until his untimely death in 1949.

Rust played a decisive role in the fight to establish the Daily Worker and is generally regarded as the paper's greatest editor, building it to

the Admiralty and confirmed by Parliament, stating that our pay will be revised, we are resolved to remain as one unit, refusing to sail under the new rate of pay.

"The men are quite agreeable to accept a cut which they consider reasonable."

Naval discipline blown sky-high in Atlantic Fleet

Led by the Repulse, the 16 ships of the Atlantic Fleet set sail for their home ports at midnight, Wednesday.

Hundreds of people waited on the shore in the darkness and watched them sail.

Whilst to all outward appearance the Fleet looked normal, the events that had taken place on board the vessels were unprecedented in modern British naval history.

For 48 hours the seamen had been on strike against the robber National Government, and during this period had refused to obey all orders.

Before the men agreed to set sail they demanded an undertaking that the ships would go to the home ports and not to an unknown

---

the very zenith of its influence, during and immediately after the Second World War.

The great Daily Worker reporter Claud Cockburn, in the second volume of his memoirs Crossing The Line, *described Rust as "the most apparently supple, and capable of being the most rigid, of Communists I have ever known." Yet, in due course, "his remarkable and at first contradictory qualities appeared quite suddenly to integrate." As well as suggesting that Rust was "a character who would have walked through the world of Brecht's Threepenny Opera with success," Cockburn acknowledges that he "often defended my attitude and actions at a good deal of discomfort and (at least once) of danger to himself. Whatever you might think of his opinions at a given moment, he was a man to go, as the saying is, tiger-shooting with."*

destination. The Admiralty assurance that their representations will be "considered" has not caused the sailors to climb down.

They are determined, in the words of their manifesto, "to remain as one unit, refusing to serve under the new rates." Whilst the Admiralty play for time, hoping thus to stem the tide of revolt, the ratings do not intend to lower their demands.

During the strike the officers were compelled to forget their ideas of naval "discipline" and to approach the ratings as equals, promising their support for the demands.

Prior to the sailing of the ships meetings were held on the foredeck, with the leaders addressing the men from gun turrets. Never has Invergordon heard such spontaneous cheers from the sea as they did on Wednesday night, as at meeting after meeting the ratings reiterated their determination to stand firm.

The men were in charge of the ships; the officers stood helplessly by.

Fatigue parties volunteered to keep the ship clean to work in the kitchens, etc, but all orders were ignored and all normal duties refused.

The officers were unable to come ashore, because the sailors refused to man the pinnaces.

When the ratings refused to weigh anchor on the Valiant, the officers and midshipmen tried to raise the anchor themselves. Immediately they were warned that as soon as one anchor was raised the men would drop the other one.

It would have gone ill with any officer who tried to interfere and they abandoned the attempt. Meanwhile the stokers checked the fires.

Another outstanding incident was the arrival of the Admiral's pinnace alongside the Hood. The bugle was blown for the men to stand to. The bugle was ignored and the pinnace greeted with loud boos.

When eventually the Admiralty message came through the men were quick to realise that the promised investigation meant nothing unless by their own action they could force the hands of the authorities.

From 7 till 11 on Wednesday evening the officers argued, but not until the latter hour would the men agree to sail. When they did it was only on the understanding that they would not relax their resistance until their demands were fully granted.

Daily Worker, Monday 21 September 1931

'Less pay – less work'

From our special correspondent, Sheerness, Sunday

The ships of the Atlantic Fleet have arrived back at their home ports.

The battleship Valiant and the battlecruiser Repulse, delayed by fog, arrived here yesterday morning about 7 o'clock.

Those men who were given week-end leave were soon on the train or bus to London, and during the afternoon there was little sign of the ships being in port, except that they could be seen lying out in the bay.

In the evening, however, many of the men came ashore and everywhere, in the pubs and clubs, in the homes of the dockyard workers and on the street corners they could be seen telling the workers of the events at Invergordon.

And everywhere the workers assured them of their support in any future action they might take. Never has there been such a united front of workers in the forces and industrial workers in Sheerness. All the old suspicions were broken down.

I talked to six or seven men from the Valiant, and from all of them I heard to the following effect: –

"They said they wanted an educated Navy. Well, they've got one. One that's too damned educated to stand any nonsense of this kind."

The Valiant men were rightly proud of their part in the affair. Theirs was the ship which was to lead the others out. Had they weakened when the order to weigh anchor was given, the glorious history of Invergordon might never have come to be written.

One sailor told me how, when they met in the naval canteen at Invergordon last Monday to decide on their course of action, an officer came in and announced that he would permit nothing that would conflict with the discipline of the Fleet, and that he was going to remain to hear what was said.

"Without a word," the sailor told me, "six or seven of the lads went up to him, carried him outside, and dumped him.

"That was the last time an officer tried any tricks," he added significantly.

Without exception the men I talked to made it clear that they did not intend to be fooled by fair words from the Admiralty. "Naval Discipline Act or not," said a three-stripe man, "they can't put 12,000 of us in irons.

"If they try any nonsense they'll have the rest of the Fleet to reckon with," he concluded.

"If these cuts are put across," said another, "they'll have to scatter the whole Fleet for months to come. Once we met the Mediterranean boys and joined forces with them, we'd all be out. But – we don't mean to let them put it across.

"We stand by every word of our manifesto and we won't serve under the cuts."

One man from the Repulse to whom I spoke told me that the crew had only been signed on September 2 at Sheerness and had hardly got together when the incidents occurred.

They had already been sent out on gunnery practice when the other ships struck, but were recalled. As soon as they reached Invergordon and learned the facts, the stokers checked down the fires and the men of the Repulse stood solid with their comrades.

A petty-officer told me that whilst the P.O.s and the warrant-officers took no part in the strike, they had been 100 per cent with the fight and, he added, "if the officers had tried any forcible suppression we should have been with the men."

The men on other ships in Sheerness showed themselves completely at one with the Atlantic Fleet ratings.

The majority of the men on the survey ship Endeavour, which is being refitted here, applied yesterday for a free discharge from the service. They were hauled up on the quarter-deck and lectured by officers, but were adamant in their attitude.

A dockyard worker told me of a significant incident on a submarine which was being prepared for refitting. A petty officer went up to a sailor and told him to put a jerk in the job he was doing, to which the A.B. returned: "Not bloody likely. Less money – less work."

In the whole town yesterday the Atlantic Fleet Strike was the sole topic of conversation among the workers. The evening showed a unity of industrial workers and Navy workers that augurs ill for British capitalism.

Daily Worker, Wednesday 23 September 1931

'No cuts at all,' say Navy men

From our special representative, Portsmouth, Tuesday

During the past three days I have learned a great deal about the inner history of the Invergordon Naval Strike. What I have learned has impressed me very greatly with the determination of the sailors and with the splendid impromptu organisation they threw up.

For instance, I asked one sailor from the Centaur about the cheers for the King. His reply gave me a very pleasant surprise. He said: "Oh, that. It was arranged beforehand and was the signal for work to stop on all ships. When we heard the cheers on the Valiant, we took them up and they passed all down the line. Two minutes later the strike was an accomplished fact."

Incidentally every man I spoke to was high in praise for the Valiant, upon whose lead the whole revolt depended. The Valiant will long be remembered in the Navy and must not be forgotten by the working-class movement as a whole.

"We have no trade union to represent us, like you chaps have," said an A.B. from the Hood. "We are not allowed to have properly elected committees from the ranks, but we bloody soon will have. It's no use going on like this."

Absolute determination was the keynote of the men's talk everywhere.

I heard how several officers had been roughly handled in the early stages, when they tried to interfere, and how one or two would have gone over the side had they not sung very low indeed after an exhibition of bullying.

On Sunday night I went on to Southsea Common, where a Labour Party meeting was in progress. Many sailors were in the crowd, but if they expected encouragement or leadership they must have been sadly disappointed. A passing reference was made to "the recent trouble in the Navy," that was all.

I took the opportunity to distribute copies of the Daily Worker to sailors in the crowd and soon got rid of the 150 copies I had. A number of the sailors came up to me and their remarks about the Daily Worker were as complimentary as they were the reverse about "the other bloody rags."

Just after MacDonald announced on Monday night that the cut would be reduced to ten per cent, I spoke to a number of men from the Warspite, and they made it clear that they were not satisfied.

Whilst the ratings realise that this concession has only been wrung from the Admiralty as a result of their militant action, they also understand it is a manoeuvre to prevent them pressing their demands further. The fact that the Committee of Inquiry does not contain a single man below commissioned rank is not lost sight of.

Daily Worker, Monday 28 September 1931

How they raided us

Friday evening… the last and busiest half-hour in the production of the Daily Worker. Six o'clock, the time for the last main batch of copy for page 1 to go to the press is near.

A story has been written on the visit of Special Branch detectives to our offices the previous evening. It is just being sub-edited when there is a clatter of feet on the stairs and a large and unmistakable "split" bursts into the room, another following at his heels.

"We're police officers," he shouts, above the tick and clatter of the tape machines, "all of you get downstairs."

The building is now swarming with Special Branch men, in the road outside stand two police vans which have brought them and in which they later remove their spoils.

Editorial, business and circulation staffs gather in the large room of our business side, guarded by a dozen detectives.

Our telephone and inquiry lad, a determined Cockney youngster, four feet high, recounts how two burly officers burst in on him, held him down and pulled the cord that opens the door leading to our offices.

Inspector Foster, who is in charge of the raid, says that he has no search warrant but that he intends none the less to make a full search.

Names and addresses are taken – even those of visitors, who have nothing to do with the business of the paper – and the staff "released" after half-an-hour's restraint.

Then the search is carried on – every drawer ransacked, every file searched, comrades' bags turned out, despite their protests.

"You've no right to search my bag without a warrant for my arrest," says one comrade. "This bag is part of the room and I'm going to search it," replies the detective. "And we'd search you, too, if we thought you had anything on you," chimes in another.

A comrade who vigorously maintains his protest is threatened with instant arrest.

The search goes on: Piles of papers and books that the Special Branch are to take away with them grow higher and higher.

Nothing is spared. The offices of the Young Communist League, which have nothing to do with the Daily Worker, are ransacked equally with ours.

Even new copies of Russia To-day, the Labour Monthly, and other periodicals, kept for sale in our circulation department, are snatched up by the Yard men.

Current cheque-books, needed for the payment of wages and accounts are taken: and likewise all the addressograph stencils used for mechanically addressing the wrappers of our postal subscribers.

Eventually the search comes to an end, and at about half-past eight the myrmidons of Inspector Foster drive off, with our papers and files.

But during Saturday they remained on watch outside our offices.

The police censorship

When I asked Detective-Inspector Foster on the evening of Friday, September 25, if he would permit the production of Saturday's issue of the Daily Worker (writes Comrade Rust), he returned the evasive answer that he intended to occupy the premises until his business was finished.

At that time the entire staff of the Daily Worker were detained in one room, and no person was allowed to enter or leave the premises.

After about 30 minutes the ban on the movements of the staff was lifted. But when I asked Foster if material could be sent over to the press, he stated that the offices of the Utopia Press Ltd were occupied by his men and all material would have to pass through their hands. "The officer in charge is an agreeable man, " he added, "and will pass anything that is not inflammatory."

Comrade R Bishop was present at this discussion and can vouch for the accuracy of the above facts.

Upon my arrival at the press I saw Detective Otley, who was in charge, and informed him that we intended to proceed with the production of page one.

The proofs of the other pages were at that time in his hands.

Otley then began to censor the paper.

A letter from a reader on page three was struck out and the heading of a report of "Tom Mann's speech" was altered to "Tom Mann speaks to Workers." Also paragraphs, sentences and words were deleted from this report.

When the proof of page one was pulled Mr R Wilkinson took a copy to Foster for his approval. The officer immediately deleted a reference to warrants being made out against persons other than Mr W T Wilkinson.

Subsequently, in my presence, Foster stated that responsibility for the contents of the paper would rest on the printer and that the police could not interfere.

This statement was two hours after Foster had given instructions for a censorship.

He did not offer to allow the replacement of the material already deleted on his instructions.

It is important to add that Foster informed me that he had no warrant empowering him to search the editorial and printing offices of the Daily Worker, but that he himself took responsibility for this act.

Any objection on the part of the Daily Worker would have to be made in court.

The police harassment of the paper continued periodically in the 1930s. The cartoon 'Protecting their jobs' was published during one such phase in 1935, when the paper's cartoonist Maro and the writer of the Worker's Notebook were the target of a lurid and bizarre anti-Red hate-mail campaign from 'The Black Pimpernel' and 'The Night Hawks'.

Maro was the pseudonym of WD Rowney – given erroneously in both Rust's The Story of the Daily Worker *and* British Volunteers for Liberty *by Bill Alexander as 'WC Rowney'. The records of the Military Academy at Sandhurst, where Rowney trained during 1917, give his forenames as William Desmond, while his obituary in the Daily Worker in 1937 also gave his correct name.*

Maro's cartoons appeared in the paper on an almost daily basis between late 1932 and 1935, and continued into 1936. They also adorned the walls of the Eagle pub in London's City Road, which had become the paper's local (rather than the 'Pig and Whistle') after the Daily Worker moved to nearby Cayton Street in 1934. "There were," according to Claud Cockburn, "rarely less than three plain-clothes men from the CID, putting their whisky down to expenses inevitably incurred in the pursuit of important political secrets such as might be expected to drop from the lips of the subversive types regularly there assembled."

The Worker's Notebook had become a regular feature of the paper by the mid-1930s and was often compiled by Walter Holmes, although Ralph Fox also contributed to it and was the name which appeared on the column when it was first given a byline in October 1935.

If the 'Notebook' figure alongside Maro in the cartoon is taken as depicting Fox, the drawing takes on a poignant light, as both Fox and Rowney were killed fighting with the Republican forces in the early months of the Spanish Civil War.

Protecting Their Jobs

It is understood that Scotland Yard, fearing that if the Black Pimpernels, Night Hawks or other creatures of prey get at us, the Special Branch will lose its job, is considering providing a bodyguard.

Ten minutes that shook the world

Bejay

What is this sound of popping that I hear? Are the kids putting crackers in the letter-box again? Nay, it is Labour bursting its bonds, with here a flip and there are a flop, as the bold, revolutionary programme of the Labour Government for the new Session becomes known to the waiting world.

Hark, do you hear it? ... ping ... pong... 'Tis wage slavery snapping its fetters; 'tis the oppressed masses shedding their shackles, as Labour's first Premier, armed with a mandate from the toiling masses, stands defiantly in the national forum and promises not to interfere with industry.

Thrones totter, tyrants tremble and despots dither, as the King's Speech rings his challenge through the land like a trumpet call to arms, promising to leave things as they are

The age of poverty and oppression is over, all but the arrangements for the next wage cut. After the bitter struggle of the century, Labour came into its own when His Majesty, looking every inch a King, entered a Parliament that looked every inch a gas-works, and opened the Session that will see the end of everything but capitalism.

The satirical Bejay column first appeared in the Daily Worker in October 1930 and was a regular Saturday feature for the next three years. The sketches, born equally of the 'class against class period' and the success of the first five-year plan in the Soviet Union, made exuberant fun of the MacDonald governments, anti-Sovietism and anti-communism. They were so popular that the early columns were reprinted as a Daily Worker pamphlet 'Bejay Calling' in June 1931. Bejay later wrote as 'Yaffle' for Reynolds News. The drawings reproduced here accompanied the original columns.

At last the workers have their Charter of Liberty; and I hope they will not try and pawn it to buy the kids some boots.

When the programme became known to the hungry millions their bond-bursting knew no bounds. The Government, they knew, had promised to do something for the unemployed, but the most any man expected was a steak and chips. None dreamed of such a munificent reward for patience as a Commission of Inquiry into the abuses of the dole.

Good fetter-snapping work was done by the promise to raise the school age, and many shackles were shed at the mention of the extension of the town-planning Acts and other revolutionary measures. But as a tyrant-trembler the Commission of Inquiry won on points.

How will history record this day of deliverance? I hope it will refer to it as Ten Minutes That Shook the World, for the phrase is my own copyright and I shall charge a fee for its use.

Never has a Government struck such a blow for the liberty of the subject since Lord Fatpocket raised the cry, "Hands off the people's food!" and reduced the tax on champagne. Never has Parliament echoed to such a challenging vindication of the rights of man since Cromwell tied the Speaker to his chair and said: "Clear away that booby."

Mind you, I expected something big in the way of a programme. As Mr MacDonald wrote the other day to the Labour candidate in the Paddedroom election, "You can present confidently to the electors the good work done by the Government for peace and disarmament, the reorganisation of industry on sound lines, and the mitigation of the lot of the unemployed…"

Some say he meant the reorganisation of the unemployed and the mitigation of industry on sound lines, but that is mere rudeness. The good work stares us in the face, particularly the reduction of the Navy by eighteen inches and the reorganisation of industry on such sound lines that labour costs have been cut down without any reduction of dividends.

As I say, I expected some pretty hot stuff. As an article in the "Daily Herald" says: "In comparison with others the Government is staggering in its efficiency." I am no veterinary surgeon, and it is not my purpose here to discuss the cure for the staggers. I merely wish to call attention to the efficiency.

No government, says the article, has done so much work in so short a time. That is true; I have estimated that Labour M.P.s cover an average of 20 miles per week by walking in and out of the lobby, and that the wind expended by Labour members in promising to help the unemployed would be sufficient to provide the motive power for 50 windmills working six hours a day for nine months. There is no avoiding these cold facts. Figures talk.

And now, after a brief rest to recover from the arduous task of refusing to repeal the Trades Disputes Act, the Government has returned to its labours, vigorous and refreshed, ready to plunge into the work of refusing something else.

Mr. MacDonald goes boldly forward.

It is gruelling work; little ye wot, ye of grosser brain, what weighty cares are his whose hand is on the helm of State, particularly when Big Business has him by the short hairs.

Nevertheless, fired with the courage that only a noble cause can give, ready to lay down his life if need be for the down-trodden toilers from whose ranks he sprang, Mr MacDonald goes boldly and unflinchingly forward to the foe and asks the Bankers' Industrial Development Company what he is to do next. Pop! There goes another fetter.

And so, comrades, the day of liberty has dawned. For 92 years, man and boy, I have worked hand and foot, teeth and trousers, for a Labour Government, and there it is, as large as life and infinitely more respectable.

Its achievement is all the reward I ask. I beg your pardon? No, I would not rather have a doughnut.

My hopes are fulfilled; it justifies the choice I made as a young man when I decided to go in for politics instead of fretwork. My dreams have come true.

And now lettest thou thy servant depart in peace, or better still, lend me 9d. to go to the pictures, for mine eyes have seen thy salvation, to say nothing of the umpteenth promise to ratify the Washington Convention for the benefit of such workers as happen to remain in work.

Let us then go forward in our victorious march, proudly following our three great champions: Mr Snowden, who made the world safe for bankers; Mr MacDonald, whose work for human progress would get him a job on any stud-farm as a breeder of racing tortoises; Mr Thomas, who taught the working man how to eat asparagus; these three – whose fame will ring down the ages as Shackle-shedding Snowden, Fetter-snapping Mac, and Jimmy the Bond-Burster.

What is this sound of scrunching I hear, as of ten thousand vegetarians eating a patent breakfast food? It is the Communists, grinding their teeth because Labour's bloodless victory has robbed them of their revolution.

Daily Worker, Saturday 7 May 1932

Parental responsibility

Bejay

I wish to say a few words about parenthood and the sanctity of the home. The capitalist press is very concerned about parental responsibility. "The Times" says: "The bad effect of State benevolence is nowhere plainer than in the relation between parent and child... As the State takes more responsibility for the child, the parent takes less... It is the children who suffer."

Parental responsibility takes a little understanding. Let me assist. A mother is said to have P.R. if she can write a cheque on her husband's bank and send one of the nurses to Harrod's to buy the child an Eton suit, four pairs of silk pyjamas and a rocking horse. But if she takes it to the municipal clinic to have its ears syringed, her maternal instinct goes right off the boil.

In Christian countries we insist on children having home influence. In England the influence is so strong that we are gradually doing without the home. The home influence would go, too, if the workers could pawn it, but I don't think they can.

To see the evil of state aid for children, you only have to compare the parental responsibility of working-class parents with that of parents of the better classes.

Parents, whose children are supported partly out of the rates, instead of out of dividends, sooner or later lose all sense of parenthood. Many a woman, whose child has had a meal provided by the Education Board, has failed to recognise it on its return and used it as a dishcloth. Many a father, after his child has been given a pill by the County M.O., has taken it out on a lead after supper, mistaking it for the whippet.

The Duchess of Atholl mentioned in this piece was well known for her involvement in anti-Soviet circles in this period. 'PAC' stood for 'Public Assistance Committee'. A pood was a measurement of weight.

But better class women are so responsible for their children that they employ others to look after them. My friend, Lady Fulfigger, is so responsible that she sees her children from 5.30 to 6.15pm every first and third Thursday. She has been known to distinguish her own children out of a dozen others of similar shape and size.

Lady Goop is so responsible that she never sees her children at all. It is said that one day, walking in Kensington Gardens, she stopped a nurse who was wheeling a pram and said: "What a beautiful child, Nurse. Whose is it?" and the nurse replied, "Lady Goop's, Madam." This only shows, doesn't it? But I forget for the moment what it shows.

You can imagine how awful it is in Russia, where the State takes all the responsibility, and all the parents have to do is to get jobs with increasing wages, and give their children enough to eat, thereby marking themselves off from Christian people.

We must not take away from the parent the responsibility for their children.

In Russia parents have no responsibility for their children at all, so God knows where the children come from. Though I hear that they are erecting an enormous electric incubator at Eggsk. Hence the revolutionary song, "Whose baby are you?"

Experiments are being made at Dhrivel University for producing synthetic young. The Second Five-year Plan, I hear, will include the non-responsible production of 500,000 by mass production. I have seen some of these children. Born in a laboratory at the age of 18 months, these darlings never knew a mother's love, nor the kind caress of the broker's man who took away the kitchen table. Ask them who ran to catch them when they fell and kissed the place to make it well, they will reply, "Workers of the world, United." Oh, it makes my heart bleed.

No tender father's guiding hand directs their faltering feet, nor lifts them on to his knees to hear the pawn ticket tick. Ask them who taught their little lips to lisp the words of simple faith, and they will reply, "Agitprop." And when they misbehave they're subjected to mass smacking by the nearest shock-brigade. No wonder the cry goes up, "How long?"

Having no mother's knee to kneel at they suck lozenges instead or go fishing for tiddlers in the Volga or the Don or the Dnieper or the Dniester, one of which, I know, is 2,400 miles long, rises in the Valdai and flows into the Caspian Sea, red with the blood of innocent tiddlers. Time was, too, when I could tell you the number of square feet in a pood.

Instead of a lullaby, the Russian baby has to listen to a gramophone reciting the 21 points of the Third International, and if it goes to sleep in the middle it is charged with deviations and cut up into cat's meat, thus starting life handicapped with what psychoanalysts call the Eatipuss Complex.

I can prove this by photographs taken on affidavit by a psychoanalyst who escaped from a cat's meat camp, and I hope to sell it on to the Duchess of Atholl for a quid.

Russians have taken away the home influence from the workers. It is true they have replaced it by bedrm., sitt., bath, h. and c., and usual offices. But there is no home influence, only electric light. They say the home influence used to give the people typhoid.

We cannot understand this, we English, who will allow nothing to invade the sanctity of the home, fourth floor back, knock twice, except the policeman, the vicar's wife, and the P.A.C. inspector. For the Englishman's home is his castle, even if he shares the midden with 15 other families.

It may be said by those who defend the evil system of State aid for working-class children, whose parents' wages would not purchase a beetle's perambulator, that the State does not, after all, do much. The Chief Medical Officer for the Board of Education backs this up. He says, "The percentage of defects established before the child enters school is steadily increasing."

So we may congratulate ourselves that our high ideal of the sanctity of parenthood is proved by the increase of infantile maladies. I think we should celebrate this by a dance at five guineas a head, and send the proceeds to the Dogs' Home.

This is a good thing, for, as "The Times" points out, it is the child who would suffer if the community prevented its diseases. And it would never do for a Christian community to cause any of these little ones to stumble (Matt., Mark, Luke, John 6. 5.'32).

We will now sing hymn No. 3 on the papers in the pews: "There is a home for little children above the bright blue sky, or slightly to the north of the Caucasus."

The M.O. for Bedford corroborates the good news. He says: "There is a proportion, say 10 per cent, of poor physique or mentality, for which little can be done... The results of civilisation... One has to realise that one cannot cure civilisation, but has to settle down to smaller tasks, for example, trying to prevent deafness by persuading a parent to get rid of a child's adenoids."

But the Russians go much further than this. They are starting to cure the results of civilisation. They are not, like Christian nations, content to cure deafness by cutting out adenoids. They have begun cutting out civilisation to cure starvation.

They said capitalist civilisation adenoid them.

Daily Worker, Monday 24 September 1934

Pit rescue work stopped At least 100 still entombed in blazing mine

Rescue operations were suspended last night at the Gresford Colliery, Wrexham, the scene of the appalling disaster of Saturday morning. The reason was that the terrible devastation wrought underground by the explosion made the work of rescue too difficult.

While accurate reports are still not forthcoming, it is certain that at least 100 men are still entombed. Rescue workers, three of whom have lost their lives in the effort to save their comrades, report that the very stones seem to be blazing beneath their feet.

Nevertheless, with unequalled heroism, miners who themselves only escaped death by a hairsbreadth are rushing to join the rescue brigades.

The Gresford colliery explosion, in which the final death toll was 264, was the worst mining disaster of the inter-war years. The report was the first contributed to the Daily Worker by Claud Cockburn, as both his memoirs and a special Morning Star supplement, published to mark the paper's 50th anniversary in 1980, make clear.

Cockburn, who had previously been a correspondent for The Times in Germany and the United States, remained on the staff of the Daily Worker until the late 1940s, using the byline 'Frank Pitcairn'. In addition, he published the political circular The Week, which did much to expose the pro-nazi elements in the British ruling class, the Munichites for whom he coined the term 'the Cliveden Set'.

The first two volumes of Cockburn's memoirs, In Time Of Trouble *and* Crossing The Line, *supply much incidental and humorous detail about life on the Daily Worker during Cockburn's years with the paper.*

Is That Damned Paper Still Coming Out?

By Our Special Representative, Wrexham, Sunday

"Ventilation was so bad in that mine that for months a lot of them worked naked except for their clogs. Every so often they had to take their clogs off to empty the sweat out of them."

That is what workers in the Wrexham district say about the condition of the Dennis Deep of the Gresford Colliery before the terrific explosion on Saturday morning, in which scores of workers lost their lives.

That is one of the damning series of hard facts behind the smoke-screen enveloping the greatest mining disaster in Britain since the war.

Here is another: On Wednesday afternoon of last week, little more than two days before the catastrophe, the workers in a section of Gresford mine near the section where the explosion actually occurred, had to be pulled out of the mine in a hurry on account of the dangerous quantity of gas in the mine.

To-day at least 100 workers are entombed in the blazing mine, where they daily sweated, half naked and in known danger for an average maximum wage for highly skilled men of less than £2 per week.

The barrier behind which they are imprisoned is still blocking rescuers nearly half a mile from the coalface, where the trapped men were working when the explosion came. "The very stones are burning," a rescue worker told me in the early hours of this morning.

The force of the explosion was so terrific that all along the main roadway leading from pit bottom to the fall blocking the road, the big structural girders are lying bent and twisted like pieces of wire.

Three of the first workers who volunteered to go to the help of their comrades were themselves killed – "gassed" as the official announcement admits. They had gas-masks, supposed to give protection, just as the National Government and the warmongers tell us "civilian gas-masks" will protect us in "the next war."

They are supposed to have monthly gas-mask practice at the Gresford Colliery. Some say they had it regularly; some say it was pretty slapdash practice.

Certainly, the men and their gas-masks had actually been tested in artificial gas-filled chambers. They had the gas-masks, they had the tests, and now they are dead – "gassed."

For eight years Gresford Colliery has had difficulty in getting local men to work there. Before the crisis began they used to have to get men from Yorkshire and South Wales.

Since the beginning of the crisis, the bosses have had the whip-hand, and the local men have had to go to Gresford. Labour Exchange and the P.A.C. and the Means Test have seen to that.

Since then coal capitalism's hit-and-run drive to profits, crashing all danger lights, has got steadily faster.

Here is what has been happening. Almost everywhere, including Gresford, electrically driven machinery has been installed and is kept running in mines known to be heavy with gas, because to stop it and use the pick or compressed air would cost the companies money.

From the gate-head switch where the main, heavily protected, cable ends there are about 200 yards to the coal face. On the coal face electric cutters, electric borers, and the conveyor belts are all run by electricity.

They are connected with the main cable by wires carrying 500 volts and protected only by thin rubber tubing. Everyone knows it is unsafe, because a slight fall of coal would cut the tube and fuse the wire, and in a gassy mine explosion is bound to follow. But though a mine is known to be gassy, the electric rush goes on.

All through Saturday big London newspapers were getting out "news" sheets as an advertisement for themselves, and selling the single pages at one penny a time to anguished people trying to find the truth and given the wildest rumours instead, at 1d a time.

The Wrexham district is swarming, too, with insurance agents from the big newspapers.

The Daily Herald insurance man told me he had to send a report to his newspaper within an hour and a half of reaching Wrexham from London.

"Why? Because they want to scoop the other papers by publishing a bigger list of insured readers than anyone else."

The huge number of the victims was to some extent the result of the miserable wages of the men. Half the men who were trapped in the mine were there that night because they wanted to go to a football match, and the only way they could do it was to work all Friday night as well as all Friday afternoon. Otherwise they would have had to lose the pay for a whole shift.

So they worked from 2.30pm to 9.30pm on the afternoon shift on Friday, and then "doubled up" with the night-shift, going on from 10.0pm to 5.30am. It was between one and two o'clock when the explosion came.

The capitalist Press and the preachers are weeping crocodile tears for the poor miners of Wrexham. At a meeting called to appeal for volunteers, one of the company speakers spoke of the necessity for experienced men. "Mining," said he, "is a high art. We want the men who have had fifteen and twenty years to master it."

Tears and admiration for the fate and the skill of the miner are running freely and come pretty cheap. Yet the same capitalist Press which is now so kind to the miners, is the Press which views with horror the demand of the South Wales men for the restoration of the 1931 cuts.

The dangers are the same, their heroism is the same. And when they demand restoration of the cuts the Press moans about the "blow" to the coal industry that a rise would involve.

In the capitalist papers and the pulpits they speak of the tragedy and the anguish of the workers of Wrexham. There is tragedy. There is anguish. There is something else, stronger than either, which the capitalist papers say less about.

That is anger, and a rising spirit of revolt against the intolerable conditions under which they live. To the bourgeois world the explosion at Gresford is an abrupt, isolated incident, like the explosion of a volcano.

To the workers it is a horrible incident in a long and frightful struggle. It is also a signal for them that "things cannot go on like this," a signal for action.

Stop press
Official statement issued last night by management, miners' agent and H.M. Inspector said owing to further explosions all entombed men must be dead. All rescue stopped.

My God! They even got the name of the sailor as well

Libel laws can be a defence for the individual – they can also be turned into an ugly weapon by which reaction and the state can hammer the radical press.

It was like that during much of the first-half of the last century.

With the number of cases brought against us during many of our first years it probably appeared the same to those at this paper in its early, beleaguered days.

But there was one which got away.

It was the day we named the sailor. The day of the Royal Wedding when, in a huge ruling class junket, the millions of hunger marching unemployed were greeted with the sight of unemployed but wealthy royals assembling from all corners of the earth.

The Maro cartoon 'Joy-day in the royal rabbit warren', satirising the nuptials of a pair of minor royals, was probably his most popular drawing.

The splash story that day, 'Out-of-work princess signs on for dole', set the context: "Today Marina, daughter of an unemployed 'Greek' ex-Prince, marries George, son of the head of the most prosperous branch of the firm of Royalty Unlimited – the Buckingham Palace branch of the old German family concern which supplies Europe with unwanted monarchs. When she signs the marriage register, Marina will qualify for the handsome dole of £25,000 a year. As a bachelor, George drew £10,000 a year. Marriage allowance will be £15,000... By forming this match, Marina has done very well for the numerous members of her branch of the Royalty Unlimited concern, who, since the war and their ejection from Russia, Greece and elsewhere, have been doing rather

Among those who joined this Royal Rabbit Warren, as cartoonist Maro termed it, was Cyril Romanov.

On the great day we carried an editorial pointing to the contrast between "the pomp, luxury and wealth that is being poured out upon two representatives of royalty, who never in their lives have done a useful thing" and the fate of the miners at Gresford.

A terrible toll of 264 lives had been taken in a pit disaster there – but the official inquiry into the accident was taking place in a room so small that few miners could attend the hearings.

Several of the guests at the wedding were dealt with by the paper – and to this day you will find in the browning pages of bound volumes of past Daily Workers the 13 paragraphs devoted to Cyril on November 29, 1934.

Our reporter explained:

"The Windsor family, thinking of Cyril's past, can scarcely sleep o'nights for fear someone will have to dash down and bail him out of Vine Street or shoo a rush of Piccadilly blondes off the doorstep.

"George Windsor's beard practically bristles with embarrassment every time he passes cousin Cyril on the stairs. For Cyril is not quite the kind of man you are glad to bring home to mother.

"Unkind persons refer to him and his wife – the Grand Duchess, you know – as the 'woman with a past and the man without a future.'

"Cyril and what our family tree refers to as his 'consort,' are gleeful. This is the first time they have been invited to London.

---

poorly. Swarms of these poor relations of the Royal Rabbit Warren are now in London, luxuriating in luscious pastures."

Among the most notorious of these was the Cyril Romanov depicted in the cartoon, which also alludes to a remark of Stalin which had been reported earlier in the year, warning the capitalist countries to keep their snouts out of the Soviet garden.

Another piece, 'Tsar Cyril embarrasses the Windsors', appeared in the same issue of the Daily Worker. The sequel, related in a special supplement for the paper's 50th anniversary in 1980, is reproduced here.

A subsequent royal engagement was marked in the Morning Star of 25 February 1981 with the prescient advice to a young, independent woman, 'Don't do it, Lady Diana'.

"The fact is that Cyril is one of those relations George would a lot rather get a nice chatty letter from than have around the house.

"He is one of the skeletons in the family cupboard, and, every time he moves, he rattles."

So far so good. It was when he came to read the next paragraph that the lawyer took fright. It had to come out, he declared.

Like all newspapers, ours has a rota of lawyers who check through everything going in for legal problems – anything from libelling a star footballer whose knobbly knees are in fact the best in the business and whose deliberate foul was nothing of the kind, through advertising a raffle to tangling with Frank Chapple of the EETPU.

Back in November 1934, the paper was written quite some way from its printer's works. The change the lawyer demanded was sent round on a "pull" of the story but got mislaid on the way. When the full pull of the whole page came back to the editorial office the paragraph was there unchanged.

By that time only emergency measures could be taken. Down a crackling phone line the instruction went: "Chisel the sailor" – the paragraph referred to a sailor.

Hopefully at the print works someone would literally take out a chisel and chip the offending lines away from the metal mould by then clamped firmly on the rollers of the printing press.

Somewhere down the line there was a misunderstanding.

Instead of a jagged white space on the page the story continued:

"The reason Cyril continues to salt the earth after being blown up on a Russian battleship in the Russo-Jap war of 1904 is Cyril's presence of mind. Struggling in the water was a sailor, and Cyril; and there was only one spar of wood to get to safety on. Cyril, realising in a flash the importance of his own life, thought it would be more prudent to be alone on that spar. Chesil, the sailor, got drowned."

Thanks to that mishearing, so the office story goes, the incumbent of Buckingham Palace could only complain in impotent anger – "Damn they got the name of the sailor as well."

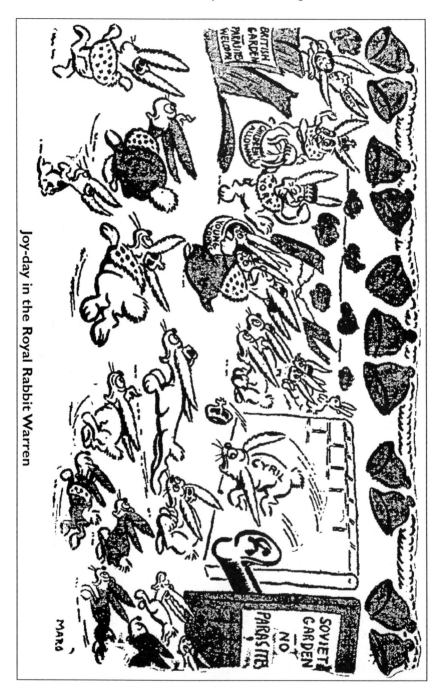

Bombers attack Emperor's mountain camp

The war as I saw it by the Daily Worker special correspondent in Abyssinia, Walter Holmes

At Kworam I saw the Emperor for the first time in the traditional role of the Abyssinian kings, as leader of his soldiers in the field. During the months at Dessie he had maintained a fairly strict seclusion, not to say inaccessibility. But once the advance to take the field against the enemy had begun, "Janhoi" (such is his ancient title) descended into the midst of his people and conversed freely with them.

Which was of great value to the observer as revealing much about the people and their relation to their ruler.

Preparations had been made at Kworam for accommodating the Emperor on the assumption that he would be the target of enemy air attacks. The assumption was amply justified, for from the day in mid-February, when his caravan left Dessie, until the return to Addis Ababa in mid-April, there was hardly a day of respite from bombardment.

So at Kworam caves had been prepared. To the south-east of Lake Ashangi runs a ridge which, from the basin of the lake itself, appears only a line of moderately high hills crowned with juniper thickets.

Walter Holmes reported on the Italian fascist invasion of Abyssinia from October 1935 until the summer of the following year, acting also as The Times correspondent at the war front. Upon his return to London at the start of June 1936, the Daily Worker published a series of accounts of his experiences.

Holmes had worked on George Lansbury's Daily Herald during its left-wing period, edited the Daily Worker's immediate forerunner, the Sunday Worker, and was one of the few staff members with journalistic experience when the Daily Worker was founded in 1930.

But ride to the top, and you will pause startled, for suddenly as you wind among rocks and trees the ground seems to fall away before you to infinite depths, and you are looking far down upon a wide plain covered with bush and to the distant ranges of the Danakil.

This remarkable mountain-face is furrowed by ravines with sheer walls of volcanic rock in which are many natural recesses and caverns. One of the deeper ravines had been chosen as the Emperor's stronghold. In its innermost wall were three great recesses like giant letter-boxes placed obliquely one below the other.

Here Haile Selassie sat in council and in state. On a small flat grassy plot above, on the very summit of the ridge, we – his two secretaries, the keeper of his horses and mules, one or two officers and myself – pitched our tents every sunset and struck them before dawn, for no tent must be left standing to catch the eye of the Italian bombers who circled unceasingly overhead from shortly after sunrise until sunset.

The Emperor himself slept nearby in a large stockaded tukul, or native house, owned by some local dignitary. Every morning, as we were hastily swallowing coffee in the chilly grey light, the hum of many voices would indicate that Janhoi was emerging from his house on his big white mule, and, surrounded by his functionaries, was riding to the edge of the ridge preparatory to descending to his caves.

Behind ran barefooted a murmuring crowd calling for blessings, for favours or merely for bread. On foot also we would follow by a shorter, steeper path to the top of the little zig-zag which led to the giant letter-boxes.

Those early morning assemblies at the caves, in the warm light of the sun rising over the distant Danakil, are an unforgettable fantasy. It was difficult to believe that it was real, grim and tragic.

He was an early Moscow correspondent for the paper and, before Abyssinia, had reported from Shanghai in 1932 on the atrocities committed by the Japanese invaders. He later covered the Nuremberg war-crimes trials for the paper, while his name became synonymous with the Worker's Notebook, which he compiled until the column ended when he retired in 1966.

On his death in 1973, the Morning Star recalled Harry Pollitt's description of him as "the father of Communist journalism in Britain."

The little Emperor, in helmet and pale khaki cloak, took his seat under a striped garden tent on a small terrace constructed outside the highest of the three caves, and hopefully camouflaged with juniper trees. Round him proud chiefs and dignitaries took up their stand.

On a small emplacement at his left hand stood his Oerlikon anti-aircraft gun mounted on a tripod.

On every accessible slope and ledge above, below, all round, multitudes gathered and pressed on each other. Some just to gaze, others to beg. Cripples and lepers mingled with soldiers crawling back from the front with weeks-old gangrened wounds, with soldiers and peasants burned by mustard gas. All squatted on the steep paths and competed as to who could evoke most pity by exposing the ghastliest horrors.

There was only one Abyssinian doctor to tackle it. A quiet, gentle little man, trained in America. He had the conventional little black bag, with a few pairs of scissors and forceps and a small supply of surgical materials. How absurd that black bag used to look on that mountainside. But the doctor worked away quietly, doing his best.

One had never contemplated this scene for more than a few minutes before the cry arose, "Airoplan mata!" – "The aeroplanes have come." The slopes and ledges would take on the appearance of a disturbed nest of ants, as the massed multitude began hastily to unpack itself and disperse in search of holes or cover.

The beautiful silvery three-engined Savoias or Capronis would shoot into the blue over the ridge three at a time, and the now familiar whistle and crash would begin, while columns of black smoke rose from among the juniper trees. More work for the little doctor. It was getting more than he could ever cope with.

Dhogossian, the Emperor's horseman, and I would lie under a rock and watch the bombs descending and guess where they would fall. When a machine appeared on a course bringing him dead over us, we would watch him fixedly through binoculars, to see if he would release a bomb which might be likely to land on our position.

Odd that we always did that, for if he had done so it would have mattered nothing whether we saw it or not.

Meanwhile, the Emperor would take his seat at the tripod of his gun and watch patiently for an Italian to fly within range. It didn't happen often, for the Fascist Air Force which, we learn from Mussolini, is to be considered as a "warning" to us, showed notable caution in keeping away from such weapons as its practically defenceless victims possessed.

No great dash about these Fascist air heroes. Had there been, they could have done far greater damage. But sometimes one would sail across the Emperor's field and would be greeted with a spurt of one-pound shells. Often the Emperor's tracer-bullets would skim thrillingly near the mark, but unfortunately never a bull's-eye.

Sometimes, as the bombers circled, we would see descending the silvery torpedo shapes of gas containers, and shortly afterwards the pungent smell of yperite, the most modern form of our old terror, mustard gas, would drift down the wind. But this was only a fore-warning of worse to come.

For some reason or other, the Italians never dropped gas into the Emperor's ravine, although they were well acquainted with its position, and the effect of gas on the work of General Headquarters would certainly have been highly disruptive.

The bombardment of Headquarters in any case marked a departure by the Italians from the unwritten convention observed, for example, in the Great War, when both sides carefully avoided such attacks. But for that there is a simple explanation. The Abyssinians had no means of retaliation.

In such conditions we sat for three weeks while the enemy, only 30 miles distant at Amba Alagi, brought up his troops and supplies, and while the Emperor considered his plans for launching the decisive counter-attack.

Daily Worker, Monday 15 June 1936

Marching Emperor leaves for decisive effort

The war as I saw it by the Daily Worker special correspondent in Abyssinia, Walter Holmes

The scene at the caves of Kworam on the night when the Emperor struck camp to advance for the last stage of his march to meet the Italians can never be forgotten by any who saw it.

Only two white men took part – Doctor John Melly and I.

Melly has already met the common fate, and I remain the only one who will ever attempt to describe the scene.

It happened that the British ambulance, of which Melly was chief, had taken the decision to retreat, in order to reorganise its bomb-shattered apparatus, just at the moment when the Emperor had resolved on his decisive counter-attack.

I had been visiting the British ambulance during the day, and at sunset, as the last trio of Italian bombers trailed away over the mauve and purple waters of Lake Ashangi, Melly and I set off on the three hours' ride to the Emperor's caves – Melly to take what proved to be his last leave of the Emperor, and I to rejoin my little private army of a score of Abyssinian muleteers and camp-boys who had vowed to remain with me whatever happened.

It was already dark as we rode down the foothills to the southern end of the lake, where the plain of Kworam lies, bounded by the easterly ridge in which were Haile Selassie's caves.

From all the bush-covered hillsides surrounding the plain were descending winding streams of twinkling points of fire.

They converged on the plain at the big mule-track which passes by the eastern side of the lake into the mountains to the north. And northward along this track there flowed a veritable river of fire.

These were warriors among whom the word had been passed that Janhoi was going to meet the enemy. They were mainly the irregular soldiers of the Emperor's Chamberlain. The Imperial Guard, numbering probably ten thousand, had moved up in something more like regular order the night before.

For many weeks we had been in the habit of marching only at night so as to give Mussolini's air heroes less chance of using their bombs and gas on defenceless men and women.

Thus there had been concentrated in the network of valleys and ravines round Kworam a mass of irregular troops – with their women, mules and donkeys – which must have numbered tens of thousands.

On our left, down the broad pass through which, in 1868, Napier had marched his column to Magdala, came an endless procession.

To our right, where the high and difficult pass to Sokota rises grim and black, the torches mounted until it was hard to distinguish them from the great stars which hang low and glittering over the mountains.

Cutting across the various streams of men, who paused to let the "ferengi" pass with a friendly salute, we steered our course through the darkness by the aid of the outlines of the farther ridge, with which I was now thoroughly familiar.

More than once my pony, a rather sensitive animal, stopped with a suddenness which nearly lost me my seat.

He had seen what was invisible to me, that bombers had been at work here, and the plain was littered with carcasses of horses or mules. A detour was necessary to get the shuddering beast to proceed.

At last we mounted the farther ridge, and came to the point where, as I described in a previous article, the mountain breaks away in a vast precipice and you look over to the distant Danakil.

But now the scene was even more remarkable. Winding among the rocks and ravines of that great mountain face were endless streams of torchlight, while there rose an unbroken, mysterious murmur of voices.

Men and mules brushed us as we halted under the dark juniper trees.

Dismounting, Melly and I led our ponies down the precipitous path to the ravine, where were the Emperor's caves. Twenty minutes of staggering and colliding with heavily laden men and animals brought us to the entrance to the caves. It was now ten o'clock.

The throng on the precarious footholds overhanging the ravine were denser than ever. Here was no ordered movement, but apparently confusion and aimless waiting.

Happening by good luck on a soldier with whom I was acquainted, I persuaded him to take charge of our animals, and Melly and I scrambled and elbowed our way up to the caves.

And there, by good luck, was Ato Wolde Gheorges, the Emperor's secretary, always unperturbed and courteous – who once said of me: "His sang-froid is terrible" – but who himself endured unceasing toil, hardship, disaster, and tragedy without ever losing his magnificent poise and reserve.

The Emperor had not yet left his caves. And in a few minutes we were led in. Haile Selassie was in his field equipment, cloaked and booted, with a woollen balaclava muffling his face under his topee.

He, Wolde Gheorges, Melly and I, stood in the midst of piles of bales of equipment and ammunition boxes while Melly, his lean length bent under the roof of the cave, explained in English the need to withdraw the ambulance for reorganisation, which speech I rendered in my best French to Wolde Gheorges, who in turn gave it in Amharic to the Emperor – who understands French, but seemed to prefer this method of interpretation.

The Emperor murmured a few words of appreciation of the work of the ambulance, and of regret that not even a few doctors could have been left in this moment of great need, and offered his hand.

His eyes were unseeing; his face was set. We had the impression of a man who felt that tragedy lay before him, but whose resolution could not be broken.

Half an hour later, Haile Selassie was riding away towards the scene of the decisive struggle, among the murmuring multitude, pressing and struggling to lay a hand on his stirrup.

At daylight, as I followed up the trail by Lake Ashangi, the three-engined bombers were already circling overhead, hurling their heaviest bombs on spots which they thought might conceal the Emperor. For their spies had already brought them news of his departure.

Daily Worker, Monday 5 October 1936

Mosley did not pass: East London routs the Fascists

Daily Worker Special Reporters

Sir Oswald Mosley's challenge to East London yesterday resulted in the most humiliating rout of the Blackshirts. The trumpeted march through Whitechapel never took place – and never looked as if it could possibly take place. Instead, the Blackshirt marchers were escorted by thousands of police from Royal Mint Street at 4 o'clock – two hours after their scheduled time of departure – away from Whitechapel, westwards, not eastwards.

They marched to the Embankment, where Mosley left them. They asked the police officer in charge for permission to go to Trafalgar Square to hold a demonstration. They were told they could march to the Square if they liked. On the way they tried to march into Downing Street, but were turned away.

On arrival at the Square the police there informed them that no

The defeat of Sir Oswald Mosley's plans to stage a fascist march through London's East End marked one of the Communist Party's most important pre-war victories. The Daily Worker played its part in the mobilisation by publishing a special four-page supplement in its London copies on the eve of the attempted march.

The Daily Worker had opposed Mosley from the start, denouncing his first manifesto for reviving British capitalism when it appeared in December 1930, signed by such left luminaries as Aneurin Bevan, AJ Cook and John Strachey. In a leading article entitled 'The British Hitler', the Daily Worker wrote: "Mosley dashes into this scene of indescribable chaos, bankruptcy, collapse and human suffering with a new set of catch phrases and capitalist remedies... The Mosley manifesto is a programme of attack on the working class to be carried through by Fascist methods."

meeting would be permitted. Several Blackshirts tried to defy the police, and a number of arrests were made. The by now thoroughly dispirited Blackshirt hordes then marched off down the Strand.

The rout of the Mosley gang was due entirely to the splendid way in which the whole of East London's working class rallied as one man (and one woman) to bar the way to the Blackshirts. Jew and Gentile, docker and garment worker, railwayman and cabinet-maker, turned out in their thousands to show that they have no use for Fascism.

The Fascists were due to assemble at Royal Mint Street at 2.30, while the Communist Party had appealed to the workers to throng Aldgate and Cable Street at 2 o'clock.

Hours beforehand every street between the Mint and Aldgate was thronged with people. Many of the side streets in this area were cordoned off by police long before the march was due to start.

No one was allowed to go through these streets unless he could satisfy the cordon officer that he had legitimate business there. The inhabitants were scarcely permitted to leave these streets at all.

In one of these streets where I managed to persuade an officer to let me through, I found a cafe packed with Blackshirts. I went in and over a cup of tea I heard one of Mosley's men and the proprietor talking. Said the former: "You can say what you like, I have had enough of being on the stones. This movement is bread and butter to me and I'm not chucking it."

At 1.30 two lone Blackshirts appeared in Royal Mint Street. They were told to stand against the wall and six policemen were detached

---

This analysis was reiterated the following year, when Mosley broke with the Labour Party to form the New Party, the forerunner of the British Union of Fascists. R Palme Dutt wrote in the Daily Worker that March: "The Mosley line is the line to Fascism and war."

As the Daily Worker consistently opposed the British Union of Fascists, an unsuccessful attempt was made to sue the paper for libel by Mosley's propaganda chief – William Joyce, later the notorious nazi traitor Lord Haw-Haw.

The Maro cartoon was drawn at the time of an earlier Mosley rally and is typical of Maro's representation of the fascist leader, who was one of his most frequent targets.

to stand in front of them, hiding them from the crowd. Shortly afterwards a covered vanload of Blackshirts appeared. As the first two men dismounted the crowd was on them before the police could intervene, and in another second both were stretched out, unconscious.

Then the police activities started in earnest. From all quarters foot and mounted police appeared on the scene. Within ten minutes there were three baton charges in Royal Mint Street, and all the while crowds were being pushed back and more streets cordoned off.

Eventually the Minories was closed entirely and the crowd pushed back half way down Cable Street. By this time Royal Mint Street itself was emptied of workers, and was occupied by about 500 police, and the assembling Fascist forces which came up mostly in closed vans.

No worker was now allowed within a quarter of a mile of the Fascist assembly place. But the workers everywhere were resisting strongly the attempts to force them off the streets which they inhabit and baton charges were repeatedly taking place in Great Alie Street, Leman Street, Cable Street and elsewhere.

Cable Street was a more than lively spot throughout the afternoon. The first incident in this sector was a baton charge at 2.20, to which the workers replied by a fusillade of stones. The outcome was three arrests, one of the arrested being a girl. All three had been hit about the head before arrest and were being dragged through the streets struggling desperately.

The crowd, infuriated, made a sudden surge forward, and after a hand-to-hand tussle succeeded in rescuing one of the men. Not only so, but the three constables who had hold of him were compelled to take refuge in a shop where the crowd imprisoned them until reinforcements came up and released them.

By this time the blood of Cable Street was up. Barricades were built in the street, and packing cases, a lorry and a couple of carts, to say nothing of the contents of a builder's yard, were called into service to build it.

Paving stones were torn up and broken into convenient sizes to serve as ammunition, glasses and bottles were broken and the splintered glass ground into the road to impede the passage of the mounted. The police tried to stop these operations, but were powerless to do so.

In the meantime Leman Street from the LNER station at the bottom end to Gardiner's Corner at the top, was also a battle ground, and I estimate something like a dozen arrests took place in that street between 2.45 and 3.15.

Many of those who were arrested had their heads cut open and faces streaming with blood. At least two policemen also had very serious face injuries from the stones flying through the air.

The police called every modern device into action to help them in their activities. Dozens of wireless vans were stationed at strategic points. Two planes were making an aerial reconnaissance, whilst from every police box plain-clothes men, who were as conspicuous as they would be inconspicuous, were keeping in touch with headquarters.

Shortly after 3.30 it became obvious that the police were going to make a desperate effort to get the Blackshirts off. Five hundred men who had been waiting in the Leman Street police yard marched out, and at the same time a similar number marched into Leman Street from the direction of Bow. From the direction they took the impression gained ground that they intended to force the Blackshirts Hounsditch way.

But whatever was the original intention, wiser counsels prevailed. It was on the orders of the Police Commissioner himself that the march was abandoned, it being obvious that to persist in it would have meant the fiercest street fighting ever witnessed in London.

The East London workers had said: "Mosley shall not pass." They showed yesterday that they meant it. One of the most impressive features was that of hundreds of thousands who thronged the streets, one could find no single person – Jew or Gentile – who was not hot in his condemnation of the Fascists and their methods.

A quarter of an hour after the parade should have moved off Sir Oswald Mosley arrived at Mint Street. Union Jacks on decorated poles rose in the air and a forest of hands above the black-coated ranks went up in salute as Sir Oswald, wearing the new Blackshirt uniform, with a peak cap, drove down the ranks in a car with two other officers of the movement.

As the car approached the outskirts of the crowd which was being held back by police, boos and cat-calls were raised and many started singing "The Red Flag" and the "Internationale."

Daily Worker, Monday 14 December 1936

Why art to-day follows politics

Virginia Woolf

I have been asked by the Artists' International Association to explain as shortly as I can why it is that the artist at present is interested, actively and genuinely, in politics. For it seems that there are some people to whom this interest is suspect.

That the writer is interested in politics needs no saying. Every publisher's list, almost every book that is now issued, brings proof of the fact.

The historian to-day is not writing about Greece and Rome in the past, but about Germany and Spain in the present; the biographer is writing lives of Hitler and Mussolini, not of Henry the Eighth and Charles Lamb; the poet introduces Communism and Fascism into his lyrics; the novelist turns from the private lives of his characters to their social surroundings and their political opinions.

Obviously the writer is in such close touch with human life that any agitation in it must change his angle of vision. Either he focusses his sight upon the immediate problem; or he brings his subject matter into relation with the present; or in some cases, so paralysed is he by the agitation of the moment that he remains silent.

The appearance of an article by Virginia Woolf in the Daily Worker illustrates the growth and breadth of the paper's influence by the end of 1936, by which time it had been an eight-page broadsheet daily for just over a year, a size it was to maintain until the outbreak of the Second World War.

Woolf contributed this specially commissioned article to a paper which was also publishing reportage by Ernest Hemingway and experimental fiction by John Dos Passos (accompanied by a brief guide on how to read it).

But why should this agitation affect the painter and the sculptor, it may be asked? He is not concerned with the feelings of his model, but with its form.

The rose and the apple have no political views. Why should he not spend his time contemplating them, as he has always done, in the cold north light that still falls through his studio window?

To answer this question is not easy, for to understand why the artist – the plastic artist – is affected by the state of society we must try to define the relations of the artist to society, and this is difficult, partly because no such definition has ever been made.

But that there is some sort of understanding between them, most people would agree; and in times of peace it may be said roughly to run as follows:

The artist on his side held that since the value of his work depended upon freedom of mind, security of person, and immunity from practical affairs – for to mix art with politics he held was to adulterate it – he was absolved from political duties; sacrificed many of the privileges that the active citizen enjoyed; and in return created what is called a work of art.

Society on its side bound itself to run the State in such a manner that it paid the artist a living wage; asked no active help from him; and considered itself repaid by those works of art which have always formed one of its chief claims to distinction.

With many lapses and breaches on both sides the contract has been kept; society has accepted the artist's work in lieu of other services, and the artist, living for the most part precariously on a pittance, has written or painted without regard for the political agitations of the moment.

Thus it would be impossible, when we read Keats, or look at the pictures of Titian and Velazquez, or listen to the music of Mozart or Bach to say what was the political condition of the age or the country in which these works were created.

And if it were otherwise – if the Ode to a Nightingale were inspired by hatred of Germany; if Bacchus and Ariadne symbolised the conquest of Abyssinia; if Figaro expounded the doctrines of Hitler we should feel cheated and imposed upon, as if, instead of bread made with flour, we were given bread made with plaster.

But if it is true that some such contract existed between the artist and society in times of peace it by no means follows that the artist is independent of society. Materially, of course, he depends upon it for his bread and butter.

Art is the first luxury to be discarded in times of stress; the artist is the first of the workers to suffer. But intellectually also he depends upon society.

Society is not only his paymaster, but his patron. If the patron becomes too busy or too distracted to exercise his critical faculty the artist will work in a vacuum and his art will suffer and perhaps perish from lack of understanding.

Again, if the patron is neither poor nor indifferent, but dictatorial – if he will only buy pictures that flatter his vanity or serve his politics – then again the artist is impeded and his work becomes worthless.

And even if there are some artists who can afford to disregard the patron, either because they have private means, or have learnt in the course of time to form their own style and to depend upon tradition, these are for the most part only the older artists, whose work is already done. Even they, however, are by no means immune.

For though it would be easy to stress the point absurdly, still it is a fact that the practice of art, far from making the artist out of touch with his kind, rather increases his sensibility.

It breeds in him a feeling for the passions and needs of mankind in the mass which the citizen whose duty it is to work for a particular country or for a particular party has no time and perhaps no need to cultivate.

Thus, even if he be ineffective, he is by no means apathetic. Perhaps, indeed, he suffers more than the active citizen because he has no obvious duty to discharge.

For such reasons then it is clear that the artist is affected as powerfully as other citizens when society is in chaos, although the disturbance affects him in different ways. His studio now is far from being a cloistered spot where he can contemplate his model or his apple in peace.

It is besieged by voices, all disturbing, some for one reason, some for another.

First there is the voice which cries: I cannot protect you; I cannot pay you. I am so tortured and distracted that I can no longer enjoy your works of art.

Then there is the voice which asks for help: Come down from your ivory tower, leave your studio, it cries, and use your gifts as doctor, as teacher, not as artist.

Again there is the voice which warns the artist that unless he can show good cause why art benefits the State he will be made to help it actively – by making airplanes, by firing guns.

And finally, there is the voice which many artists in other countries have already heard and had to obey – the voice which proclaims that the artist is the servant of the politician.

You shall only practise your art, it says, at our bidding. Paint us pictures, carve us statues that glorify our gospels. Celebrate fascism; celebrate Communism. Preach what we bid you preach. On no other terms shall you exist.

With all these voices crying and conflicting in his ears, how can the artist still remain at peace in his studio contemplating his model or his apple in the cold light that comes through the studio window?

He is forced to take part in politics: he must form himself into societies like the Artists' International Association.

Two causes of supreme importance to him are in peril. The first is his own survival: the other is the survival of his art.

"While very glad to print this article by Virginia Woolf in our pages, we must, of course, point out that it is not entirely our view she expresses.

"We doubt whether artists in the past have been so peacefully immune from the conditions and issues of the society in which they live as she suggests, and we feel sure that we can learn quite a lot about "the political condition of the age or country" in which Titian, Velazquez, Mozart or Bach, lived by examining the works which they have left us." – Daily Worker Editorial Note.

Mr Orwell will have to try again

The Road to Wigan Pier by George Orwell, reviewed by Harry Pollitt

Poor old Wigan! What things have been done in your name! From bad music-hall jokes to literary gents trying to hang their pegs around your name. The great thing is that we who come from Lancashire long ago learned to laugh at it all, in a way those who try to raise the laughs would never understand.

Here is George Orwell, a disillusioned little middle-class boy who, seeing through imperialism, decided to discover what Socialism has to offer.

What a tragedy that a man can give up a position that the best years of his life were spent trying to fit him for, and then at a crisis in his life not see the real way to go.

Fortunately, Orwell has the sense to admit his own ignorance. He tells us: "But I knew nothing about working-class conditions..."

"When I thought of poverty, I thought of it in terms of brute starvation. Therefore my mind turned immediately towards the extreme

---

In The Road to Wigan Pier, *George Orwell acknowledged: "As for the working class themselves, they have gained immensely in economic knowledge. I believe that the Daily Worker has accomplished a great deal here: its influence is out of all proportion to its circulation."*

When Harry Pollitt, the general secretary of the Communist Party, reviewed this contribution to the Left Book Club series, Orwell had yet to embark fully on his career as an anti-communist writer. Orwell's biographer Bernard Crick refers to this review, but gives readers of his book, George Orwell: A Life, *no inkling of the real thrust of Pollitt's critique – that Orwell understood little of the socialist movement and the new trends forming the Popular Front against fascism and war, to which Pollitt's review indicates the paper's positive response.*

cases, the social outcasts, tramps, beggars, criminals, prostitutes. These people were 'the lowest of the low,' and these were the people with whom I wanted to get in contact."

It is perhaps natural that a late imperialist policeman should only see "the lowest of the low," as the place from which to get his new understanding of social conditions and Socialism. But, of course, it was completely wrong, and must be responsible for the terribly distorted view that the author seems to have of everything connected with the working-class movement.

I suspect he knows nothing about this at all.

What a pity to travel all the way from Mandalay to disguise yourself as a tramp who can get into a Limehouse lodging-house without betraying his middle-class accent.

If ever snobbery had its hallmark placed upon it, it is by Mr Orwell.

If on his return from Mandalay he had bought one or two penny pamphlets on Socialism and the working-class movement, what fatal experiences he could have saved himself from. Because one never gets to know the movement by slumming.

The result of the author's mirage is a completely false picture and wrong conclusions, that have nothing in common either with the working-class or the Bloomsbury types that Mr Orwell so fiercely tilts against.

I gather that the chief thing that worries Mr Orwell is the "smell" of the working-class, for smells seem to occupy the major portion of the book. Well, pardon me if I say at once, without any working-class snobbery, that it's a lie. But if one comes to smells and one tries to formulate one's political outlook on this basis, dear me, the aroma around Pall Mall on debutante night, or in the theatre train to Golders Green, only makes me more of a Bolshie than ever.

But Mr Orwell has missed the real Lancashire. This is the real tragedy of his young life. Now at the youthful age of thirty-four he has been through it all and seen nothing and learnt nothing.

The Lancashire homes of shining brass, gleaming steel, of clean curtains and stoned doorsteps and back yards, the spotlessly clean homes of a working-class that were the backbone of the Chartist movement, that formed some of the first trade unions, that conducted historic fights for free speech long years before Orwell was born;

the Lancashire working-class that were amongst the first to break with Liberal Labourism, that were amongst the first to return Labour members to local councils and to Parliament: this is the Lancashire that Orwell has missed, and in missing has lost tremendous opportunities for making a valuable contribution to the literature of our time.

Similarly with his diatribes against "bearded fruit-juice drinkers" (and I am not one of these), yet I cannot refrain from saying that when Orwell deals with this section of the population and fondly believes he is tilting against those who are coming towards Socialism, again we have the same distorted picture.

He misses the new ferment and political awakening that is taking place among important sections of people, who are coming to politics for the first time: who are really concerned with the crisis in present-day society: who are anxiously wanting to find a way out: who in a hundred and one ways are now beginning to make their contributions to various aspects of the working-class movement.

I am not concerned whether a man wants to drink a lemonade with a straw and in shorts or whether coming out of the docks he calls for a pint of Mann and Crossman's: the thing I am concerned about is: are they concerned to try and build up a new society? If so, what is the best way in which we can help them?

And we don't do this by telling them they "smell," or that they are "showing fat bottoms in shorts." It can only be done by patient argument, by careful explanation, and by really trying to understand their particular problems, and show by our understanding that we want to help.

We won't win anyone to Socialism by knocking hell out of Huxley's "Brave New World," and then building another conception of one that is even worse.

Mr Orwell will have to make another attempt, and really try to learn himself before he takes on the role of a new up-to-date Socialist mentor and professor. And if he works as hard at this as some of those his fiercest criticism is levelled against, he may even become qualified to use his pen later on to win other people to Socialism.

James Maxton will appreciate the fact that it is not my role to defend the ILP. But nothing in this book so completely gives its author away as his description of an ILP branch meeting.

I am sure that just as most Lancashire women who read this book would like to dust Orwell's pants for his insults and delicate nose, so workers who give their time and energy in trying to build up the Labour movement will feel the same when they read some of the descriptions of working-class activity.

Is there nothing good about the book? There is. The description of a miner getting to the coal face is superb. It will bring home to thousands of members of the Left Book Club what the miners' work is really like. It will convince thousands that something ought to be done for the miners who would never be convinced by a miner himself, for they would think he was putting "the paint on a little too thickly."

The indictment of housing in many of our industrial centres is also a good piece of work which will surely have an effect in discussion circles, and attract them to support every campaign directed towards better housing and social conditions.

If Mr Orwell had stuck to this last, and his camera, confined himself to fighting against these things, then he would have rendered a great service to the people who are now campaigning for improved conditions for the workers.

His book is certain to arouse discussion and controversy. I know it has taken me all my time to write in this fatherly way about it.

But if it warns people against the danger of seeing a tramp or a young man with a beard or a student in sandals, and then setting oneself up as an expert on Socialism, it will perhaps have not been in vain.

If it warns those people genuinely trying to find their way to Socialism, that they won't find it by peering into middens and chamber pots, but by hard work inside those organisations that strive to improve immediate conditions; by deep study of the history of the Labour movement; by study of Marxism; then their own creative work will be of a much higher level than that of the author of "The Road to Wigan Pier."

One thing I am certain of, and it is this – if Mr Orwell could only hear what the Left Book circles will say about this book, then he would make a resolution never to write again on any subject that he does not understand.

Daily Worker, Saturday 27 March 1937

The epic of Arganda Bridge

This is the story of the battle for the Arganda Bridge. It is the story of the heroic struggle on that vital area of the Madrid front, Jarama Sector, where the first International People's Army met and defeated the military machine of Fascism. It is the story, too, of the magnificent part played in that battle by the English-speaking Battalion.

It is told to the Daily Worker by two men whose record as fighters and as political instructors will live as long as the history of the Spanish civil war is known – DF Springhall, organiser of the London Communist Party, and Peter Kerrigan, organiser of the Scottish Communist Party.

Kerrigan and Springhall returned to London last week. They were

---

This report of the battle now known as Jarama Valley was probably the first sustained account of the legendary action of the British Battalion of the International Brigade in defending the Madrid front against overwhelming odds. Arganda Bridge was a nearby location to which the paper's splash on 6 March, 'Epic of Anglo-Irish battalion in Madrid's battle', had referred.

That splash had been based on a letter from Peter Kerrigan to Harry Pollitt. Both Kerrigan and DF 'Dave' Springhall acted as political commissars with the International Brigade and both held a variety of senior positions in the British Communist Party. In addition, Springhall acted as editor of the Daily Worker for a period around 1938, while Kerrigan acted as Daily Worker correspondent in Spain later during the war. Other Daily Worker correspondents in Spain included Frank Pitcairn (Claud Cockburn), William Rust and Sam Russell.

Bill Alexander wrote of Jarama Valley in British Volunteers for Liberty, *the history of the British Battalion in Spain, that "the posi-*

full of enthusiasm for the magnificent fight that is being carried on by the International Brigade and the Spanish People's Army.

Springhall quiet, calm and cheerful, carried on his cheek the scar of a wound received during the hottest period of the long battle – a scar which shows how miraculous was his escape from mortal injury. Kerrigan was luckily unwounded, but has returned somewhat thinner, his hair greyer.

They spoke of deeds which have added a new and glorious page to the history of the English-speaking people. Of men who fought unrelieved for days against bitter odds; of a glorious march which saved a battle at a time when the issue wavered. Of creation of a new type of army, the like of which the world has never known.

Springhall, leaving London for Spain last December, found that new army in the process of formation. Men from every country in the world, from Britain and Ireland, from France and Germany, from America and Italy, from a dozen other countries, were welding themselves into an efficient fighting force inspired by one great purpose – the defeat of Fascism, the preservation of democracy, the consolidation of forces which will yet change society.

In a village near Albacete the English-speaking battalion was in training. It was a training which was of necessity hurried, for times were critical and men were needed. In the space of several weeks men had to undergo the training which took several months during the great war. But men who are eager to learn and know why

---

tions taken up by the British Brigaders and their allies in this great recovery remained unchanged and intact until the very last days of the war. Even then these positions did not fall by assault."

Alexander's roll of honour of those volunteers who fell in battle in Spain lists over 160 who were killed at Jarama Valley, out of a battalion strength of some 500. Among the dead was Desmond Rowney, the Daily Worker cartoonist Maro – one of four members of the paper's staff killed fighting for the Republican cause. The others were the reporter Ralph Fox, who died at Cordoba in December 1936; George Hardy, a printworker, who was killed in Aragon in March 1938; and Walter Tapsell, the paper's business manager and a political commissar in Spain, who was killed in an ambush at Calceite in April 1938.

they must can acquire knowledge quickly. Leaders were already appearing.

"One of the men who first attracted our attention," said Springhall, "was Jock Cunningham, now commander of the English-speaking Battalion. We regarded him as one of our most promising military leaders, and he was marked for promotion. When Captain Nathan was promoted after the fighting at Cordoba, Jock took his place, and still later took over the command when Wilfred Macartney was wounded.

"Training was intensive. Evening courses, which were voluntary, were held in machine-gun instruction; rifle practice was continuous. Macartney was responsible for organising training in every branch of infantry warfare.

"The Battalion was composed of men of many shades of political opinion, from members of the Communist Party to Liberals. They had one great bond of unity – a determination to resist Fascism to the death.

"There was a large number of men from the Labour Party and the Socialist League, many of whom were secretaries of ward, local and divisional parties, and, of course, the percentage of trade unionists was very high. All these men maintained contact with their parties and with their trade union branches.

"They did more. They sent a combined resolution to the British Labour leaders at Transport House, condemning the official Labour policy towards Spain and demanding an immediate campaign to aid the Spanish people.

"The Battalion, as part of the International Brigade, formed an integral part of the Spanish People's Army, and these two combined were something that has never been known before – an International People's Army, an army which had undertaken the great task of defeating Fascism and defending democracy.

"And in other ways this army was unique. The whole English-speaking battalion, like other battalions, periodically held battalion meetings on methods of training, on objectives, and the many expressions of opinion and suggestions made at these meetings contributed to an increase in military proficiency.

"When the battalion needed a club-room, the United Socialist

Youth organisation placed their premises at our disposal, where there were books, newspapers and a wall-newspaper, which was very popular. There were social gatherings of various kinds together with the villagers, and a highly successful Burns night was celebrated.

"Our relations with the local population were excellent. The Mayor and the local Popular Front Committee worked unceasingly to make us comfortable and to give us help in every possible way.

"We held joint meetings with the villagers and with the youth movement. Our comrades were invited into the people's homes to supper. In addition to this, members of the Battalion collected for the civilian sufferers in the war several thousand pesetas. This was contributed entirely from the men's pay of six pesetas a day.

"The district was not free from secret agents of Franco's 'Fifth Column,' but because of our cordial relations with the Spanish people, the 'Fifth Column' propaganda had no chance. Fascist agents did their best to spread the lie that our men were mercenaries and ruffians, the riff-raff of Europe.

"The villagers knew better. They knew us and we knew them; they were solidly behind us.

"During this period an important factor was the visit of the London Trade Union delegation. The entire village, headed by a brass band, turned out to give the delegation a great welcome.

"It was because of all these factors – the political consciousness of our men, their eagerness to attain maximum military knowledge, their feeling that they belonged to a People's Army and were themselves helping to build up that army, the support they had from the population – that they were able later to prove themselves more than a match for the highly trained and better armed professional soldiers of the Fascist invading army.

"This was the background of the English-speaking Battalion of the International Brigade. Soon the time came when we received orders to move up to the Jarama front in company with French, German and other battalions.

"We went up to the front on February 12. Even as we were moving up the Italians were taking Malaga and beginning that massacre which has shocked and outraged the entire world. But of those events we then knew nothing.

"News of Malaga's fall had, however, reached the Fascist troops at Jarama. The result was that all along the front the Fascist morale was high. They believed they had at last succeeded in making a definite advance and optimistically believed that they, too, could take the initiative on the Jarama sector and cut the vital Madrid-Valencia road.

"The Fascists held strong positions. They had control of the key bridge in this area and occupied the most advantageous heights.

"The Fascists believed that they could not only force us from the positions we had moved up to occupy, but also that they could advance to take possession of heights in our rear, which dominated the approaches to Madrid, including the Madrid-Valencia road.

"If they accomplished these aims they would complete the encircling movement around the capital that they had been striving to accomplish for so long.

"The Fascist general had given his troops three days to achieve their objectives. The Moors and Spanish Fascists who composed the enemy forces at this point had been promised extra pay and leave if they succeeded in their attack.

"It was in these circumstances that our Battalion went into action on February 12. In the very first moment of the battle we had an additional handicap. We had no time to dig trenches and were forced to use whatever natural cover we could find, taking advantage of the olive groves and certain rises in the ground.

"The Fascists immediately opened a large scale offensive. With airplanes, artillery, machine guns, bombs and rifle fire they battered at our lines.

"Our boys fought back magnificently. Time after time they beat off waves of Moors and Spanish Fascists. Remember that for a great number of men in the Battalion this was their first baptism of fire.

"During this first day we lost a number of our best comrades, among whom was Bill Briskey, a very popular Company Commander, who had been a London bus driver.

"With dawn on the second day the Fascists launched a second attack even fiercer than the first. Our food and water supplies had been unable to reach our lines. The men had neither eaten nor slept, and only on the third day was it possible to bring up supplies and get some rest. Hungry and tired, they held on grimly, while the Moors and Fascists pressed furiously against them, concentrating every effort on the achievement of their aim.

"But eventually numbers and superior equipment began to tell. The Fascists were particularly strong in machine-guns. Our men were obliged to fall back a little and the battalion suffered a heavy loss when Tom Wintringham, our Commandant, was carried away wounded in the thigh. Wintringham's place was taken by Jock Cunningham.

"On this day our aeroplanes brought down two Fascist machines in flames and did magnificent work.

"During the third day the Fascists were able to force a retreat in the sector held by the Spanish comrades. This led later in the day to a general retirement, a large part of the English-speaking Battalion having to retreat through the olive groves.

"Again machine-gun fire took a heavy toll along our whole front, while we were inadequately equipped with these weapons. Here was to be seen the concrete and terrible results of the embargo on arms for the Government forces.

"The tale of non-intervention was that day told in blood and wounds. Men who might still be alive died that afternoon as the victims of the policy of the National Government and the Labour leaders.

"The fascists at this time were pressing forward vigorously, making every possible use of their superiority in arms and numbers. Their aim was to transform a retreat into a rout. But though conscript Italians may flee in disorder, having little faith in their battle, volunteer fighters for democracy do not.

"Nevertheless, the retreat continued, and for a while it looked almost as though the Fascists might achieve their objectives in the time they had set themselves."

Here Springhall paused. And here indeed was the most critical and vital moment of his story. The episode of which he then spoke is one which will stand to the eternal glory of the British working-class movement for as long as men can remember or speak.

It is an episode which may well have been one of the turning points in European history.

"It was at this moment – 4 o'clock in the afternoon of the third day of the battle – that the general commanding our forces gave orders that at all costs the retreating troops must hold a certain ridge abutting on the main road and make a new line to prevent further Fascist advance.

"And it was here that the English-speaking Battalion distinguished itself particularly. Our men had become somewhat scattered, like that of other battalions. The Battalion reformed itself in two halves, one led by Cunningham, and the other by Fred Copeman, well known for his part in the Invergordon mutiny.

"From two different points the battalion marched along the road towards the vital ridge singing the International.

"Their escape was infectious and largely decisive.

"Others from other battalions – French, Belgian, Spanish, rallied around and joined in – and all of them together moved rapidly up in excellent order to the required position. They had to move across open country under heavy fire to reach the ridge, but their aim was achieved, the ridge was held. The enemy advance was checked.

"From that moment the battle took an entirely different turn. When dusk fell, the men of our battalion, using their own initiative, did not limit themselves to holding the ridge, but led the way in a determined counter-attack.

"The counter-attack was pressed home along the whole front. In face of this the enemy wavered, broke, and then fled in disorganised retreat at a far greater rate than their advance had been. Their losses were estimated as being heavier than our total losses during the whole of their three-day attack.

"Later that night our forces were able to take up position in their original line, or to within 300 to 400 yards of those positions. During the night we entrenched ourselves in good positions.

"During the following days the battle consisted of almost unceasing attack and counter-attack. When we stopped, they began; when their attack ceased, we replied. There were continual artillery bombardments, and air raids were frequent. The strain of this period was intense and almost without intermission, either by day or night.

"Our men, with comrades from other sections of the International Brigade, went over the top time after time singing the International to launch fierce and sustained attacks on the enemy positions.

"During this period some of our machine-gunners when ordered to retire refused to carry out the order and insisted on continuing to use up their remaining ammunition on the Fascists, against whom they had a clear and deadly field of fire. Unfortunately, this reckless heroism resulted in some of these comrades being killed.

"Though we suffered relatively heavy losses during this period, which lasted until February 21, the Fascist losses were enormously heavier. Our continuous attacks had the effect of exhausting the Fascists and greatly lowering their morale.

"This became obvious round about February 20, when the number and power of their counter-attacks began to diminish greatly. Sometimes when they had a chance of following up an attack and gaining valuable ground, they were unable to do so. This fact was recognised by us and confirmed by the prisoners and deserters who were brought into our lines.

"From February 21 we began to take the initiative, forcing the Fascists on to the defensive and gaining ground, which was quickly consolidated and entrenched."

Dogs howl in empty Almeria, people hide in caves – Nazis came

From Frank Pitcairn, Valencia, Wednesday

Last night I stood at a window in Almeria and listened. Absolute silence except for first one and then another dog. The dogs ran about the streets looking for food.

Madrid and Valencia are silent at night, but that is a different sort of silence. By an incident of small magnitude you are aware of hundreds of thousands of people all around you, you can hear them breathing. Almeria at night is dead. 65,000 people lived there before the war. Tonight there are not many more than 1,000 in the whole city. The Nazis have driven them out.

Above the city you can see the ancient Roman ruins, and you begin to understand what the Romans felt like when the barbarians came.

Supposing this were Southampton or Dover. Most of the population wandering about in the New Forest or the Downs, looking for a comfortable cave to settle down in; thousands of others coming into

---

Claud Cockburn reported from Spain, under the byline Frank Pitcairn, from the earliest days of Franco's fascist revolt against the Republic. Two days after the Daily Worker had headlined the news 'Fascists land troops on Spanish coast', Cockburn filed a front-page report from Barcelona on 22 July 1936. Many of his despatches, filed mainly over the next 12 months, were collected in Cockburn In Spain *edited by James Pettifer. Cockburn's own immediate impressions of the war were published in the autumn of 1936 in his book* Reporter In Spain.

On the same front page as this evocative report appeared, the paper gave notice of its tipster Cayton's first success in the Derby, the 100-7

town every morning early and leaving again at night – for fear the Nazis should come again.

There is still a certain amount of work for civilians to do in Almeria. For instance, the first man I saw at work in the morning was the coffin-maker, who is busy already and expects to be busier still. Is this, you wonder, really the state of things to come?

The big construction works in the city is something that looks as though it were going to be an underground railway. It turned out to be a vast system of subterranean bomb-proof refuges and passages for the civilians from the Germans when they next put the principles of totalitarian war into practice.

During the daytime you can in many parts of the town have the illusion that nothing at all has happened. You would expect to see something tremendously spectacular. On the contrary, things look what we have taken to calling 'normal'.

For instance, there is the facade of the Hotel Simon. It looks all right. Nothing has happened there you think. Then you step inside and find that one quarter of the roof has been shattered by a German shell and the rest of the roof is falling down at intervals in small showers of tile and plaster.

Over there is the civilian hospital. It appears untouched. You go upstairs and find that where the back ward was there is literally nothing left.

There were no sick people there for the reason that at one o'clock in the morning there was an air-raid alarm signal and, the Germans

---

shot Mid-Day Sun. Cayton (Alf Rubin) had started giving racing tips in the Daily Worker in September 1935 and continued to contribute tips to the paper for 60 years until his death in December 1995. He won the Sporting Life naps competition four times, a joint record, and would have scored on several more occasions had the paper not been excluded from entering for many years.

Cayton became renowned for his long-priced successes, epitomised by the 66-1 winner of the 1949 Grand National, Russian Hero. But when he was asked in a 1995 interview which tip had given him most pleasure, Cayton replied unhesitatingly: "Mid-Day Sun. They laughed – they were all clever boys. But the damned thing won the Derby."

being the way they are about hospitals, the invalids were brought downstairs.

They lay in the passageway some two hours later listening to the shells go whistling methodically into this quarter and the rest of the city.

The shells fired systematically, directed by the German Admiral, reached that street. One shell blew the back of the hospital to bits. The next ripped open the roof of San Sebastian church, the third, scheduled by the Nazis for that section of the city, hit the street just beyond.

Two burst in the air above the street, spraying shrapnel on to the houses within reach. They also fired shrapnel shells into the other streets. This was a good idea of the Germans since people who ran out from the houses had a good chance of being killed by shrapnel in the open streets.

I met a young doctor, a very normal person, looking like an average young doctor of a large provincial town. His name is Lewis Criada. What happened to the Criada family is typical of what happened to people in Almeria when the Nazis ran up the battleflag.

Lewis Criada himself was working at the military hospital. A shell fell in the garden. All over the town great puffs of smoke and thick clouds of red brick dust began to come up until they hung over the place like a cloud.

The ambulance men driving through the fire of shells began dashing up with wounded. Then when they started to operate they found the water, electricity and gas had all been cut off by the shelling.

Meantime, Criada's old mother and father had been asleep in their bedroom on the second floor of a block of little flats on rising ground just behind the centre of the town.

The shutters were closed. They were awakened in the darkness by the whistling of the shells and the crashing all around. They dared not open the shutters to see what was happening.

Like thousands of other families in Almeria that morning they cowered together in a corner of the room imagining, as people do in such a situation, that the corner would somehow be safer than anywhere else. They clung to one another for protection.

Then a shell exploded on the third floor and then they blew up the whole top of the house and buried the old couple down below in masses of plaster and broken glass.

Five seconds later a shell fell in Criada's own bedroom, fortunately empty, because he was working at the hospital.

Finally, at almost the same moment, the house in which Criada's sister lived across the street, Majadores Street, had its roof and part of its back wall smashed by another shell.

Just one family and all in less than an hour.

And the town, as I said, looked almost normal.

All along the main streets houses are pitted with shrapnel holes. Shells had exploded in the middle of the street making it as wide as Oxford Street – shrapnel holes two and three inches thick in the walls. They blew scores of holes through the iron shutters of shops. Nobody who was in that street when the Germans started up had any chance of escaping unmaimed.

When there is an air raid there usually come warnings. On this occasion the German fleet took care there should be no warning.

If the people in Almeria had not been fooled so often they might believe that now at last the democratic powers are going to act to keep them safe from the German guns. They do not believe it. They believe that the People's Army and the magnificent Navy and Air Force of the Republic are already upon the road to final victory and peaceful Spain.

In the meantime, they do what their Roman forefathers did when they, too, were in danger of being attacked by wild beasts. They leave the city at night and go to the hills and live in caves in the rocks.

In the hotel where I stayed only three people had remained for the night. The waitresses had gone to the hills at five in the afternoon. Before they went they put in a dozen of the rooms a few scraps of meat and cold fish in case soldiers or other travellers on business should turn up and have to spend the night.

We ate one of these meals by candlelight and listened to the dogs howling in the empty street. This is Europe in 1937 ...

Daily Worker, Thursday 3 June 1937

We gave the Derby winner

By the Sports Editor

Cayton, the Daily Worker racing correspondent, again came up trumps yesterday, when Mid-Day Sun, his tip for the Derby stakes, flashed past the post as the winner at 100 to 7. This triumph is all the more significant since we were the only national daily newspaper to select the winner…

Immediately the result of the Derby became known we had many telephone calls of congratulations. One East London worker tells us that the Daily Worker tip, the winner Mid-Day Sun, was given at East London meetings, and as a result of this selection many East London workers had "done themselves a bit of good."

In addition, many copies of the Daily Worker were sold on Wednesday morning on the paper's Derby selection.

Morning Star, 3 June 1981

My days at the Daily Worker

Claud Cockburn

Misled, probably, by sensational literature and the motion pictures, people said one thing was certain, and that was that it would be very, very different from The Times. They said they could hardly imagine a bigger change than going from The Times to work for the Daily Worker. Like most statements made without fear of successful contradiction, this one turned out to be full of error.

True, the plain-clothes detectives of the Special Branch of the CID, bulging in the saloon bar just across the street, struck a note unusual in Printing House Square. So did the social viewpoint of the cartoons presented to the publican by a former artist of the paper in payment for services rendered.

Then I noticed the expression on the face of the van-driver waiting to rush next day's paper to the stations, and became aware of something at once rare and familiar. I had seen it in the faces of Times drivers, but – until now – nowhere else.

It was an expession which said the edition was going to come off the press long behind schedule, and he was going to risk his neck tearing along the streets to Euston and Paddington, and if he caught the trains at all it was going to be a flaming miracle. And just why was the paper going to be late? Not, you could bet your life, because a big murder story broke at the last minute, or floods menaced thousands, or heiress's secret wedding exclusive, or any of that class of caper, but because the leader-writer – the flaming leader-writer, well, I ask you

---

Claud Cockburn included these observations on his time at the Daily Worker in the first volume of his memoirs, Crossing The Line. *The passage appeared in the Morning Star when Cockburn's reminiscences were republished in 1981.*

– was still batting out a pronouncement on something or other and they were holding the whole edition for him while he reached the mot flaming juste.

A nice state of affairs in the middle of the twentieth century. Who did he think he was? Gladstone?

Within the building, at the entrance to the editorial offices, the sense of familiarity, of deja vu, deepened. This was not entirely due to the fact that at that date the offices of both newspapers looked, in contrast to Fleet Street, like something Dickens had set out to describe, and then left to be continued by someone who was just starting to read up on this new-fangled steel construction you heard about. Functional they were not. They reminded me of Boston. But, more than this, it was an organisational detail which evoked a memory of Printing House Square.

Naturally, all newspapers have guardians whose business it is to prevent eager but irrelevant people from bursting in and disturbing the editorial inmates at their tasks. At The Times when I worked there, this protection had been considered particularly important. And I had been told that as for the Daily Worker I should find it guarded, they said, like a fortress.

Of course, the character of the most probable intruders differed, up to a point, in each case. The Times, I had always been given to understand, was protecting the editorial staff against the onset of people with plans to reorganise the Church of England, people who wanted to publish a five-column letter demanding State subsidies for otter-hunting, and people who were going to beat up the racing correspondent because of the ruinously misleading thing he foreshadowed about the third race at Newmarket.

At the Daily Worker the job of the man on the door was rather to keep out people with plans to reorganise the Communist Party, people who wanted to get a five-column letter published demanding State subsidies for Esperanto, and people who were going to beat up the racing correspondent because of the ruinously misleading thing he foreshadowed about the fourth race at Wolverhampton.

First time I called at The Times, I got right to the editor's door without being questioned, and learned that the obvious reason for that must have been that the person who kept people out had had to slip away for a minute to make some tea. At the Daily Worker the arrangements were, in truth, more elaborate. There was a cubby-hole for the guardian to sit in, and a small guichet for him to peer out of, and a door which would open only when he was satisfied and pulled a string. On this occasion the door had been wedged open with a piece of wood, the cubby-hole was empty, and as one walked unchallenged up the stairs one caught, at the end of a passage, a glimpse of the guardian's back as he pored over a gas-ring, making some tea.

On the voyage to the interior, other well-remembered sights were witnessed. That man, half-crazed by worry and frustration, shouting about trains leaving and peering over his shoulder towards the leader-writer's room with the mixed rage and awe of one who is trying to get an archdeacon to step on the gas, must obviously be the manager. These chaps, eruditely discussing in a mood of high-minded levity the racial composition of the Saar and that business about the MCC, can be none other than the Foreign Editor and the Diplomatic Correspondent. And clearly the tense-looking man scribbling away at the end of the table is the world's greatest expert on something and, though ostensibly sub-editing a small item of late news, is really writing a definitive article for a quarterly or monthly review.

After all this, the sight of the leader-writer himself, a Scotsman, it need hardly be said, or at any rate one of nature's Scotsmen, came as no surprise at all. One had seen virtually the same man coolly holding up production of The Times while his sinewy pen wrestled mightily with Unrighteousness, a spiritual descendant of Covenanters and of the sort of preacher who held that if a full and proper exposition of the Word was going to cause the sermon to go on for five hours, then five hours was what the sermon was going to go on for. Feather-pates might babble of parishioners falling exhausted in the aisles, or trains leaving the termini without the paper. That was just too bad about the parishioners and the disappointed readers.

Occasionally, in those early days at the Daily Worker, the readers at the far end of the long-distance lines would get together in protest, claiming that they would rather have a paper with a political howler in paragraph four of the leader than no paper at all. These explosions shook the building. Campaigns were initiated for more hustle, modernity and snappy popular journalism all round. People sat gazing sadly at the Daily Express, with a view to imitating it. Over the problem of how to get snappier there raged discussions comparable to those at The Times office when some ruthless modernist, shouting for the Common Touch and plenty of it, came in with that shockingly vulgar suggestion about sticking in a crossword puzzle.

In the midst of one of these periods of controversy, I came down to the office to find a big section of the library space occupied by a broodingly thoughtful Burman, the entire table before him covered with books, brochures and manuscript documents. It looked as though the article he was evidently going to write on the situation in Burma was going to cover the subject pretty comprehensively. Next day he was still there, writing down figures in long columns – statistics of rice production, I supposed. His books and papers now took up so much room that it was hard to move about the library at all. It seemed as if it was going to be quite a series of articles. And about all this research there was something impressive and solemn, making one feel that any other article written for the paper was going to look trivial and superficial.

On the third day I took alarm and placed the whole question squarely before the editor.

I yielded, I said, to no one in my appreciation of the gravity and world importance of the situation in Burma. A couple of rousing pieces about it were, I did most profoundly realise, what the paper needed as badly as anything. But, so far as I could judge, our friend aimed at turning out a minimum of twenty such articles, and frankly, and without in any way seeking to minimise the vital urgency of getting the facts in front of the public, was the project entirely in line with decisions recently taken about developing more zing, zip and popular appeal? Would a series of twenty articles on Burma Today be the snappiest thing imaginable? As a circulation-getter, was it just what the Daily Express would do?

The editor, who personally would rather have enjoyed reading twenty longish articles subjecting the Burmese situation to an exhaustive analysis, listened with an air of melancholy. Painfully, as if revealing that in the rush for the Common Touch we had decided to go in for some kind of pornography, he explained the position. The

Burman was not, in fact, writing an article about Burma. He was not an expert on that country. What he was an expert on was greyhound racing. And what he was doing with all those books and papers was working out greyhound form for the coming season. Thereafter a section of the paper was going to be devoted to greyhound tips and greyhound results.

So, indeed, it came to pass. People who were expecting a piece denouncing the Bank of England and found instead a bit tipping Blazing Killarney Boy for the White City were disgusted, and wrote letters saying this could never have happened in the Old Days and the Tolpuddle Martyrs were rolling in their graves. Others were delighted, for however shaky he may have been on Burma, as a dog-tipster he was the tops. In the raw financial blizzard which blew continuously though the office for months on end, he was a big comfort to the staff. Perhaps if the Moscow Gold other people wrote about had really existed one would not have bothered so much about what was going to happen at the tracks. Things being as they were, Blazing Killarney Boy was worth a whole lot of imaginary roubles.

The real Britain is on the Ebro

Spain revisited, by Harry Pollitt

We set off to find the British Battalion. Through the night, till dawn comes, and soon the sun is blazing down.

The fascists boast of their love of country, of nationalism and love of people. Strange how, in Spain, they have clothed it with death, mutilation and hunger. And this – not with their own strength and courage, but with foreign Fascist intervention, the symbols of which we already see in the clear blue sky as Savoias, Heinkels and Messerschmidt bombers and fighters go mercilessly on their way.

We come to Mora d'Ebro and Mora la Nova. What ghastliness meets the eye. Not a house or building left standing. But the bombers go on. Thud, thud, thud – you hear it miles away. Later, other fascist planes come and drop leaflets – "Surrender."

They are torn up in scorn. Soldiers shake their fists at the sky. Fists are no match for bombs, but, behind the fist is that unconquerable spirit that can never be crushed.

The civilians have long been evacuated from these two villages, that is to say those who were not killed by the Fascist bombs. We stop and look around. The stench from dead bodies and mules is frightful. Here in a little garden, or what is left of it, is a rose tree in full bloom. It looks so lovely in the midst of such desolation – but its perfume vies in vain with the stench surrounding it.

And here is a kid about 10 years old, with a brush in his hand, sweeping away the dust and dirt thrown up by the last bombs. He has hardly got the steps clean, when the roar of planes is here again, and then a mad rush for safety. His family refuse to go away.

We pass through another village. Bombed to bits. Again this terrible smell of rotting human bodies and mules. I'm speechless, but vomit at what I see and feel. Round the bend of the only street, when the bombers are here again, we throw ourselves on the ground and wait. And there in a field is a mule, going round and round, turning the little irrigation buckets that water the fields.

I watch it, fascinated. Overhead the engines of death, looking like great black birds. Here we are hugging Mother Earth, away to the right of us a peasant, his wife and two children doing the same, no time to stop that mule. Round and round it goes. To give life to the vine, while from above death strikes.

Off we go again. It's a race against time to cross a certain pontoon over the Ebro. We get across. One hour later, a direct hit from a bomber and up that pontoon goes.

Now we are nearing Corbera. We can see the shells from the heavy Fascist artillery passing into the town. It's a lovely Sunday morning.

I think of Britain. At this moment in church and chapel, priest and parson are no doubt telling of God's goodness and the glory of His work. Some perchance are chanting, "Suffer little children to come unto Me."

As I looked at these shells, saw the clouds of dust and debris rise to the skies, some little children perhaps were going – in bits and pieces. They might have been yours and mine, and then what would we feel like doing?

It was at this moment I caught the look on the face of the comrade who was driving our car. The tears were streaming down his face, his fists tightly clenched. He explained he had been born in these parts. When the Fascists had captured a village in this area, his mother and sister were hiding in a cellar. The Fascists shot them.

Nobody spoke. What was there to say? We had come through miles of entrancing country. On all sides the vineyards, thickset with green and black grapes, row after row of fig trees, nectarines, nuts, apples... All waiting to be gathered in, but no hands to do it. A year's backbreaking work in the fields now come to harvest. Toil and sweat all in vain. The peasantry gone.

From dawn to dusk up the Ebro Valley – only the Fascist bombers. The only harvester – Death. Who was it who once said: "There is a Reaper whose name is Death"?

In Britain, soon the harvest festivals in Church and Chapel. Congregations raising their voices –

"Come, ye thankful people, come
Raise the song of harvest home.
All is safely gathered in
Ere the winter storms begin."

or listening to a parson say: –

"Lift up your eyes and look on the fields
For they are white already to harvest."

Let us hope they will think of Spain.

At last we found the British Battalion. Peter Kerrigan has told you all about it. I can add but little. I can never forget, however, as we climbed down the hillside and saw the comrades, the look of surprise on their faces as though I had dropped from the skies. Bob Cooney disperses any sense of the supernatural by saying, "Told you when I saw that notice in the Daily Worker about sending letters to King Street, that Pollitt was coming."

The comrades had just come out of the front line, after one of their most terrible nights, having been under fire from trench mortars the whole time. Clothing torn to shreds, a fortnight's beards on. It was difficult to make out who was who.

The thought flashed through my mind: "If only the whole of these comrades could stand on the platform at the Trades Union Congress just as they are now. No words or speeches would be needed. The delegates would rise in their wrath and take such action as would either force Chamberlain to alter his policy or throw him out of office."

One of the first things I saw on my return to London was a photograph of Clem Attlee, MP, paddling in the sea with his daughter somewhere in North Wales. It was a happy picture.

The No. 1 Company of the British battalion, to which Major Attlee gave his name last autumn, have waded through blood. Not many of them are left now. They have rendered eternal honour to Clem Attlee, seeing in him the leader of the Labour Party. Many will never embrace their loved ones again, or paddle with their children.

Is it too much to ask that the Labour Party should follow up the Trades Union Congress by holding an emergency conference of its own to help Republican Spain?

Is it too much to ask the Labour Party and the Trades Union

Congress now to give more direct help in maintaining the families of these comrades, or getting jobs for those who have returned from Spain, or to organise the sending of foodships to Republican Spain?

For the British Battalion is the real Britain. It is a deathless host. Its work, heroism and sacrifice is the only redeeming feature in the shameful history of Britain's relations with Republican Spain since July, 1936.

These men, who, in those scorching days were the first to cross the Ebro in the quickest and most efficient manner; who, alongside their Spanish comrades, handled rifle and machine-gun the sun had made like red-hot iron – they are ours. Unknown, no big names, from back street and factory – they will live for ever. Can we ever prove worthy of them all? This is the question that their work, not their wishes, puts to you and me.

The cartoonist Gabriel (James Friel) joined the Daily Worker in 1936, becoming over the next 20 years one of the greatest cartoonists of the 20th century. Gabriel's 'Mustn't wake the babies,' appearing on 27 November 1937 after a visit by Lord Halifax to Hitler at Berchtesgaden, grimly foretold the annexation of Austria and Czechoslovakia by nazi Germany, while 'His majesty's foreign secretaries,' published in the Daily Worker on 23 February 1938, exposed the pro-fascist line of appeasement after the intrigues which forced Anthony Eden out of the Foreign Office.

Gabriel left the Daily Worker in 1956, in disagreement with the paper's line on the Soviet intervention in Hungary, after the editor refused to publish a cartoon he had drawn equating those events with the tripartite aggression against Egypt.

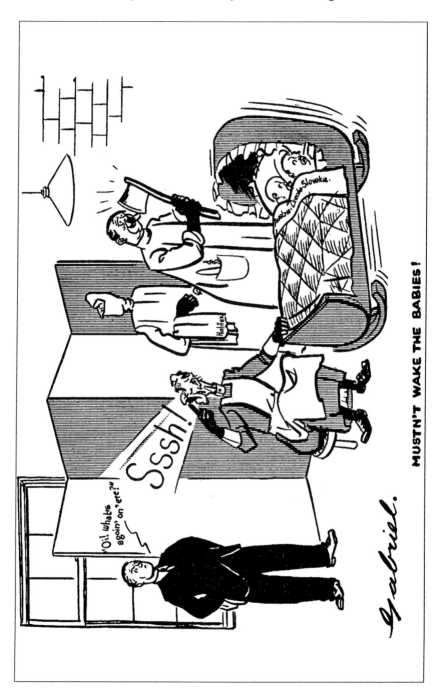

Daily Worker, Saturday 22 April 1939

You have received your death sentence

JBS Haldane

In his career at the Home Office, in Ireland, and in Bengal, Sir John Anderson doubtless approved of a number of death sentences. But until this month he had never condemned thousands of people to death by a single stroke of the pen. This in effect is what he has done in his reply to the Finsbury Borough Council in which he refuses approval for their scheme of air raid shelters. You may very well be one of his victims.

The scheme is rejected on four main grounds. First, it is said that steel shelters and propped basements are good enough. Good enough for you and me, that is to say. The Cabinet is to have "an

Professor JBS Haldane contributed articles on science to the Daily Worker from the late 1930s until the late 1940s. He was an authority on genetics, but his range of topics reflected the interests of a polymath – his own obituary, which he penned 10 months before his death in 1964, was headlined 'I've always been something of a dabbler' when it appeared in the Daily Worker in December of that year. A collection of his early articles for the paper was published in 1939, entitled Science And Everyday Life.

Haldane became a wartime scientific adviser on defence matters, but his advice on air-raid protection was disregarded until the Second World War exposed the inadequacy of Anderson's precautions. Haldane's name became synonymous with the kind of reinforced, deep shelter he advocated.

Haldane also played an important role as chairman of the Daily Worker editorial board, whose members also included the dramatist Sean O'Casey, in leading the fight to lift the ban imposed on the paper from 1941 to 1942.

impregnable battle headquarters," and the royal family, the "key men" of the BBC and a few others, are also to go underground.

Secondly, it is claimed that not all the inhabitants of Finsbury could get to shelter within the period of warning of an air raid. Certainly invalids and babies could not. Until I read the Home Office letter I thought they were to be evacuated. The period of warning is supposed to be seven to ten minutes. An able-bodied man or woman can get their boots on and walk or run 400 yards within seven minutes, and no one is to be farther than 400 yards from the nearest shelter.

If the government thinks we shall only get two or three minutes warning then, of course, there will have to be more shelters, each holding fewer people. But if so we ought to be told that the official figures are wrong.

Thirdly, we are told that the number of people catered for could not get into the shelters in the time. Certainly the time calculated is less than that allowed by the LCC for theatres. But the entrances to the shelters are roads sloping gently downwards, whereas theatres and cinemas have steps, which slow down the rate of motion very greatly.

Finally three venerable consulting engineers (one of whom has just died at the age of 70) reject the scheme on technical grounds. "Although we understand that the structure has been designed to withstand general purpose bombs of 10cwt each, we do not feel that it could be guaranteed to resist them."

These gentlemen rely on their feelings. If you design a bridge you do not rely on your feelings to decide whether it will support a four-ton lorry. You rely on exact measurements and calculations.

Now one or other of two things is true. Either the government has made experiments on the effect of heavy bombs or it has not. If it has, by keeping them secret, it makes proper shelter design impossible. If it has not it is criminally negligent. Modern war is scientific, and modern science is experimental. Sir John Anderson does not appear to realise these facts, and if we value our lives we shall turn him out in favour of someone who does.

Other criticisms are based on sheer ignorance. "We have never heard," say the experts, "of such a method as roughening the surface of one piece of concrete in order to transmit considerable stress from it to another one." And yet this principle is common in the design of jetties, which have to stand up to the sudden shock of waves.

They do not like the design, and say it would not work.

However, they admit "that this type of structure could be safely built provided that the design were radically amended. It should be noted, however, that the necessary amendments would add considerably to the structural cost of the proposals." The answer to this is simple.

A big contractor has made a firm tender to build a shelter for 10 per cent less than the cost estimated by Messrs Tecton. The more expensive method recommended by the Home Office would put up the cost 8 per cent above the estimate, that is to say by £10 10s per head to £11 7s.

Fortunately the Finsbury Borough Council realises that the government's promise of protection is worth about as much as their promises of protection to the Abyssinians and Czechs. So they are going ahead with their work, and a shelter is to be made at Busaco Street. As soon as the main entrances are ready an experiment is to be made to discover just how long it takes 7,000 people to get into it. There are 7,000 people in the neighbourhood who are very keen to make the experiment.

Is your municipality as progressive as that of Finsbury? Too often even a council with a Labour majority takes the view that it can do nothing without Home Office support. Finsbury is making history. Other boroughs can do the same.

But don't think the government is doing nothing about underground shelter during air raids. They are. Undertakers have been made a reserved occupation. I only differ from their policy on one minor point. I would sooner pay £11 to get underground before I am dead than afterwards.

I have no doubt that six months hence the propped basement will be universally admitted to be as useless as the gas-proof room recommended last September, and everyone will agree that deep shelters are essential. But in six months we may be at war. The Finsbury shelters can be completed in eight months, and even after one month will give partial protection to a thousand people.

Daily Worker, Thursday 18 May 1939

This is a sensational article

JBS Haldane

This is a sensational article. I am sorry. In these articles I try to keep to facts. But occasionally facts are sensational.

A discovery has just been made which may revolutionise human life as completely as the steam engine, and much more quickly. The odds are against its doing so, but not more than ten to one, if so much. So it is worth writing about it.

In the Daily Worker of March 1939, I described the recent work on splitting the nuclei of uranium atoms. A certain number of them explode when neutrons collide with them.

Neutrons are among the so-called elementary particles, that is to say, particles which have not yet been broken up, such as electrons, protons, and perhaps a few others. This does not mean that they will never be broken up.

Ordinary atoms hold together when they collide at a speed of about a mile a second, as they do in air. When the temperature is raised,

---

JBS Haldane's article on the new atomic science was described by William Rust in The Story of the Daily Worker *as having sounded "a grave warning as to the way in which science was being pressed into the service of war and the first indication in the popular press of those trends in scientific research which were to culminate in the dropping of the atom bombs at Hiroshima and Nagasaki in August 1945."*

The article was reprinted in the Daily Worker in December 1964 after Haldane's death, along with an assessment by Jim Jeffery, reader in crystallography at the University of London: "This article, which Haldane rightly called sensational, is a remarkable tribute to the wide range of his interests and to his ability to grasp the implications of discoveries in a subject far removed from his own speciality. Almost all the

and the speed of collisions goes up to ten miles or so a second they cannot hold together, but electrons, that is to say, elementary particles with a negative charge, are torn off them.

That is why flame conducts electricity.

But at moderate speeds, say a few thousand miles per second, collisions only break up the atoms temporarily. They soon pick up their lost electrons. When the speed rises to tens or hundreds of thousands of miles per second the nuclei, or cores of the atoms are sometimes broken up.

When a current is passed through the heavy variety of hydrogen at a voltage of half a million or so, the atomic nuclei become formidable projectiles, and if they hit a light metal called lithium they break up its atomic nuclei and let neutrons loose.

Neutrons can penetrate the nuclei of many atoms even when moving slowly, and cause still further changes.

Generally they only chip a piece off. But when they attack uranium, an element which is unstable anyway, and produces radium, though very slowly, when left to itself, the uranium nuclei split up.

The new fact, first discovered by Joliot and his colleagues in Paris, is that when the uranium nucleus splits it produces neutrons also. In the experiments so far made, very small pieces of uranium were used.

So most of the neutrons, which can penetrate even metals for some distance, get out. But if the neutrons are liberated in the middle of a

---

aspects of atomic energy and the bomb, which one thought of as not being known until the publication of the Smyth Report in 1945, are dealt with... At the time very few, even among the experts in the field, could see as far as the biologist, Haldane... The Second World War started a few months after he wrote this article and vast scientific resources were devoted to the development of the atom bomb for use in war. His fear that the discovery would be used for killing proved only too true. His further prophecy that 'owners of uranium ores will make vast fortunes' has also come true; and the fact, which he points out, that the Belgian Congo contains such mines has more to do with the operations of white mercenaries and Belgian paratroops than alleged 'mercy missions' or the 'restoration of law and order'."

sufficiently large lump of uranium, they will cause further nuclei to break up, and the process will spread.

The principle involved is quite simple. A single stick burns with difficulty, because most of the heat gets away. But a large pile of sticks will blaze, even if most of them are damp.

Nobody knows how large a lump of uranium is needed before it begins to set itself alight, so to say. But experiments are already under way in two British and one German laboratory to my knowledge, and doubtless in others in America, the Soviet Union, and elsewhere.

In the current number of "Nature", Joliot and Halban, a French and German physicist working together in Paris, published an SOS letter suggesting means for slowing the process down, so as to avoid disaster.

If the experiment succeeds several things may happen.

The change may take place slowly, the metal gradually warming up. It may occur fairly quickly, in which case there will be a mild explosion, and the lump would fly apart into vapour before one atom in a million has been affected.

Or there may be a really big explosion. For if about one four-hundredth of the mass of the exploding uranium is converted into energy, as seems to be probable, an ounce would produce enough heat to boil about a thousand tons of water. So an ounce of uranium, if it exploded suddenly, would be equivalent to over a hundred tons of high explosive.

Of course no one will begin with an ounce. Still they may do a good deal of damage. Most probably, however, nothing much will happen.

It may be for example, that the majority of uranium atoms are stable, and only one of the several isotopes (as the different sorts of atom in the same element are called) is explosive. If so, it would take several years to separate the isotopes.

Nevertheless, the next few months may see the problems solved in principle. If so, power will be available in vast quantities. There will be a colossal economic crisis in capitalist countries.

There is plenty of uranium in different parts of the world, notably in northern Canada, the Belgian Congo, Czechoslovakia, and in several parts of the Soviet Union.

So the owners of uranium will make vast fortunes, and millions of coal miners will be thrown out of work. The Soviet Union will adopt the new energy source on a vast scale, but the rest of the world will have a much tougher job to do so.

Fortunately, uranium bombs cannot at once be adapted for war, as the apparatus needed is very heavy and also very delicate, so it cannot at present be dropped from an aeroplane.

But doubtless uranium will used for killing in some way.

Any intelligent reader may well ask why, if uranium is so explosive, under certain conditions, explosions do not occur in nature. The answer is that uranium does not occur in nature in a pure state. It is generally found combined with oxygen, and neutrons would be stopped by the oxygen atoms to such an extent that an explosion could not possibly spread.

I repeat that this article is highly speculative. I am prepared to bet against immediate "success" in these experiments. Nevertheless, some of the world's ablest physicists are hard at work on the problem. And the time has gone past when the ordinary man and woman can neglect what they are doing.

Daily Worker, Friday 26 July 1940

People's own raid warnings save lives

Frank Pitcairn, Somewhere in South Wales

Several times a week German planes fly about 180 miles from France and bomb South Wales. The Government told South Wales people "it won't happen here." It is happening here.

Daily, nightly, men, women, children risk their lives because the Government failed to provide proper shelters, refuses to provide proper warnings.

The censor will not allow me to say what the effects of this Government shelter and siren policy are. The working people know only too well. Some learned it too late.

By quick and grim experience people here are learning what protection of the people really means.

When you sit night after night in a rickety garden coalshed, as people do here, with the bomber up above and no siren sounded because it might "interfere with production" on the night shift in the nearby factory, and nowhere else to go because the sacred rights of

---

The change in the line of the Communist Party at the start of the Second World War, from supporting the war as an anti-fascist struggle to opposing it as an inter-imperialist conflict, has been well chronicled and was reflected in the Daily Worker. Editorials on 'How to win the war' and 'August 1914, September 1939', on 4 and 5 September 1939 respectively, gave way to the statement by the paper's editorial board published on 30 September, 'A people's government could secure a lasting peace', followed by 'The job of the people today', signed by William Rust on 16 October. A revealing account of the change of line can be found in About Turn: The British Communist Party and the Second World War, *published in 1990 – a verbatim record of the central committee meetings which debated these questions.*

property prevent even the derelict works down the road being broken up to provide shelter material, you get quite a slant on the character of the Government.

When you have, as people have here, the choice of either letting a seven-year-old child walk a mile through a dangerous area to a school without a shelter, or seeing its education stop, you get quite a picture of the Government's "concern for the future."

When a police official comes around, as they have done here, and tells you that demands for shelters and decent protection for school children are "sinister Communist propaganda," you are apt to take an interest in the Communist Party.

People in South Wales are very much alive to the meaning of protection – alive and kicking. They are getting into action. They are taking matters into their own hands – the only hands where it is safe. They are getting things done – despite neglect and downright obstruction (I could use a harsher word).

On a hillside in the night, with a bomber throbbing on high, bombs thudding at long intervals somewhere not far off, and the anti-aircraft guns blazing away at another plane in the distance, I saw a little bit of the South Wales people's struggle for protection.

This string of typical villages lies exposed in the middle of a vast industrial area. Or rather, between two different sorts of industrial area.

All its menfolk work in neighbouring factories and plants and

---

Two themes dominated the paper's coverage of the early stages of the war. One was the drive to expose Chamberlain and the rest of the 'men of Munich' – expressed most forcefully in the editorial 'Bring the guilty to account!', published on 18 June 1940 after the surrender of Petain in France. The other was summed up in the slogan at the head of the editorial each day, "For a People's Government that will defend the people and lead forward to peace and a free Socialist Britain."

The government's failure to provide adequate air-raid defences was one of the paper's strongest campaigning issues, as this report by Claud Cockburn makes clear. The consequences of that neglect are shown in the report which follows of the first day of the nazi blitz on London.

collieries, except those already in the Army. (A little string of Union Jacks and French flags, perhaps saved from the Jubilee celebrations, is stretched across the street between two poor cottages, in welcome to a soldier back from Dunkirk).

At the very beginning of the war the best-known workers in the place applied to work in ARP. But the best-known workers in the place turned out to be Communists, or "associated with Communists." Dangerous agitators.

So the authorities engaged in "protecting" us against Hitlerism turned them down.

When the bombings started there were no shelters in the whole place. A few Andersons were secured with difficulty. The majority of the people still had nothing.

The "dangerous red agitators" got busy. A popular committee was elected.

The committee decided that if the Government would not provide shelters, the committee, with the people behind it, would simply take over the lower part of the post office and the cellar of the biggest public house, and turn them into shelters.

They did it. I saw these filled with people – men, women and sleeping children, sitting on rough wooden beams by the light of a candle stuck on the wall.

But how can the people get to the shelters in time when the Government often refuses to sound the sirens, although bombers are overhead?

They took me up on the hillside and showed me a triumph of popular organisation.

The committee has discovered that from two points on the hillside it is possible in the night to see two distant lights. They have discovered that whenever the authorities have themselves had a "yellow" warning, these lights go out.

So the watchmen of the people's committee – the local workers taking it by rota – have established observation posts. They have a tent up there and every night from 11 to 3 they do sentry-go, watching those lights.

When the lights go out, the watchers run to the village, blow their whistles, knock on the doors, lead the people to the shelters. Often no sirens are sounded at all, although the bombs sound all right. Other times the siren sounds an hour after the bomber is overhead. Or the "All Clear" sounds when the bomber is still overhead. (So as to get production going in the factories.)

That happened the night I was there. The all clear went when the anti-aircraft guns were still visibly firing.

But they didn't fool the local lads. We stood on the high bank of a lane, watching the guns firing and listening to the plane overhead, and others ran down to the shelters to warn the people not to be taken in – not to go home yet.

That happens night after night. Because there is no bumbledom and bureaucracy here, because this whole affair is run by the workers for the workers, things run efficiently and even gaily, despite the dangers.

Not that the Government gave up without a struggle. They actually had the nerve to send the police up to the hill to order the watchers not to sound their whistles or knock at doors unless the official sirens went.

What the local lads said and did to the bearers of these threats is not suitable for print.

Anyway, it seems to have been effective. Not a single official of this kind has been seen in this sector ever since. The people explain to me: "They can't come here messing things up. This place is run by our committee. We're in charge here."

And that is how, despite all difficulties and obstructions, the workers in this section are getting some measure of that protection which the Government refuses to give.

Government admits 1,700 dead and wounded

Londoners yesterday afternoon were still digging their dead and wounded out of the wreckage of their unprotected homes after the biggest raid upon Britain since the beginning of the war.

Four hundred dead, between 1,300 and 1,400 badly wounded, were the figures admitted even by the notoriously "cheerful" official communique as a preliminary estimate of the casualties in London.

A partial survey of one part of London by Daily Worker reporters yesterday seemed to indicate that the preliminary official estimate will have to be seriously revised.

Yesterday afternoon in the little streets where the houses have been smashed flat to the ground, weary rescue squads and firemen, whose work has already saved many lives, were doing their utmost to keep down a casualty roll, already inflated by lack of adequate shelter.

Whole areas had neither gas nor water, so that the usual Sunday dinner and even a cup of tea has been denied them.

In many of the streets the only shelter available had been brick surface shelters with no roofs. In others these brick boxes had been torn apart by the blast of high explosive bombs. In another area a bomb worked havoc in a shelter which was no more than a strutted basement.

When a new warning went just after midday, the talk in the shelters was of action to secure better shelter in the future.

Berliners also suffered heavily from the fury of the air war yesterday. For nearly three hours the RAF bombers spread fire and the wreckage of high explosive bombs in west and north-west Berlin.

The list of objectives attacked – including power stations, railways and industrial plants – was very similar to that of objectives attacked by the German bombers in London.

The German government officially announced that the heavy raid on London was in the nature of a reprisal for earlier British attacks on Berlin and the killing and wounding of civilians in other parts of Germany, too.

It is, of course, obvious that in any "game" of mutual reprisals between the two capitals, the numerical superiority of the German air force and the geographical position of the two Powers, is likely to tell heavily in favour of the Germans.

From almost the beginning of Saturday afternoon's London raid it was obvious to everyone that yet a new stage in the murderous intensification of the war between the two imperial Governments had begun.

People in the streets, some of whom claimed to be able to see with the naked eye the large German bomber squadrons coming over in formation, soon realised that this was something new in raid violence.

A little later the smell of burning goods and buildings was floating up across the London bridges all the way from the docks to the West. And to the East of the City vast fires could be seen leaping up into the darkening sky, with enormous "mushrooms" of mauve and black and grey smoke towering overhead.

Protection proved inadequate

Fred Pateman

Yesterday I walked through the valley of the Shadow of Death – the little streets of London's East End. In these streets incendiary and high-explosive bombs have caused widespread devastation.

One area has a whole row of streets in every one of which some building has been blasted or burned out by the bombings of the previous 24 hours. Another has a square of houses smashed almost level to the ground.

As I stood watching the weary rescuers toiling to save those still living from underneath the debris, a woman came out of a nearby house with a baby's bottle of milk and a flask of tea to be passed down to a family the rescuers were trying to reach.

Along the main roads that run through the bombed areas is a steady stream of refugees – men with suitcases, women with bundles, children with their pillows and their own cot covers – homeless in the heart of London.

Where were they going? They were going to stay with friends or relatives whose houses were still habitable although still in the danger zone.

Whatever schemes the local authorities may have had for dealing with the refugees, they did not seem to be operating very well, for everywhere I asked what had become of the folk who lived in the smashed houses and little shops, I was told they had gone to stay with friends.

In one badly bombed area stands an old building whose basements were air raid shelters in the last war. This time too they were being used as shelters.

Yesterday, when I got there, the building was cordoned off. Home Guards kept people away.

Far down in one of those basements yesterday morning people had died when a bomb struck the building above it.

Yet, as one woman who was there told me, this had been regarded as the safest shelter in the district, and people had come from many streets around to sleep there in peace.

And, in fact, it was the safest shelter near, for the only alternative was little brick surface shelters, many of them roofless, which line all these little streets.

Where was she to go last night?

That was the problem of her and all the other people in the district. And in the groups that stood around and wrestled with it there was bitter recognition of the class distinction between shelter and protection which can be seen in the East End and the West End.

Many of these women have had experience of organisation in the rent strikes that swept East London about two years ago.

Today they are remembering the great victories organisation won for them then.

They are beginning to discuss similar organised action to secure adequate air-raid protection for themselves and their families.

When the air-raid sirens sounded just after midday I took shelter in a block of tenements where one of the first and one of the greatest victories of the rent strikes was won.

The talk turned to the total lack of protection in the streets around. There was rapid consultation in various parts of the shelter.

There and then it was decided that a petition would be prepared and circulated right through the borough demanding shelters of the Haldane type. The local Communist Party, which played a big part in the rent strikes, is going to lend the tenants its help again.

Already it is getting some leaflets on the Haldane shelter so that the people can see for themselves the kind of protection they are fighting for.

Now people have seen the walls of little brick surface shelters cracked by blasts from bombs they are not going to tolerate this playing with the lives of the people any longer.

Large parts of the area were deprived of gas and water yesterday. Those whose houses were still standing were deprived of the Sunday roast, for many of them the only really good meal of the week, and even a cup of tea.

Wasn't it possible to make some emergency arrangement at the local schools or with the bakehouses for people who went through hell the previous night to have a decent meal? I am sure it was not beyond possibility if the local ARP chiefs had based their plans on the well-being of the people.

And again the lesson of Birmingham was repeated. Most of the local authorities still lack the barest minimum scheme for aiding the homeless. The heartbreaking trek to safety goes on uncared-for even in the heart of London.

The growing influence of the Communist Party and the Daily Worker – culminating in the success of the broad-based People's Convention, which met on 12 January 1941 and agreed a peace programme – led to the suppression of the paper under defence regulation 2D on 21 January. The order was signed by Herbert Morrison, the Labour Home Secretary and Minister of Home Security.

William Rust, addressing the Communist Party's central committee on 2 October 1939, had warned: "What has happened to the French Party is an idea that is running through the minds of the ruling class in this country... We know the bitter hatred in the minds of the Second International leaders towards the Communist International and our Party, and so whatever they may say in public about democracy and so forth, I am quite sure that we cannot rely on the leaders of the Labour Party to make a stand against any attack that will come on the Communist Party in this country. They might welcome it, they might even foment it if they thought we were getting too dangerous in the development of our activities."

As Allen Hutt, who completed The Story of the Daily Worker *after Rust's death, wrote of the ban: "For the next nineteen months the Daily Worker, as a newspaper, did not exist; yet as a political force, temporarily disembodied though it might be, it grew in potency and influence with every week that passed. The fight against the ban made the Daily Worker a household word throughout the labour movement, and in many circles outside. Mr Morrison and his Transport House and Tory cronies found themselves in the grip of a contradiction from which there was no escape. The more they hardened their hearts and clung obstinately to the ban, hoping that they would thus strangle for good the clear Communist voice of the advanced working people, the wider the sympathetic echoes that voice evoked. Never before in British history had a newspaper been kept out of action for so long by mere ministerial diktat. And yet assuredly the result was far other than that for which the suppressors hoped. The period of the ban brought the Daily Worker a wider sympathy and support than it had ever known and paved the way for its subsequent development into a front-rank popular national newspaper of the working class."*

Morrison was challenged to bring specific charges against the Daily Worker and was unable to do so. His action was intended as a warning to cow the press in general – the editors of the other national newspapers were all summoned to hear Morrison announce the suppression of the Daily Worker.

A few illegal issues were produced immediately after the paper was suppressed, but the decision was made early to mount a broad-based, nationwide campaign to get the ban lifted, based on the Daily Worker

Defence Leagues. Alongside this, a news agency issuing a daily bulletin entitled Industrial and General Information was established.

The Daily Worker's premises and press at Cayton Street were bombed and totally destroyed by fire in April 1941. Ernie Pountney, the paper's advertising manager, recorded in his memoirs For The Socialist Cause *that 44 tons of newsprint were saved from the fire. This scarce wartime resource was pressed into service producing campaign materials against the ban. These included five news sheets showing what the Daily Worker would have been like if allowed to publish, under the various titles Workers Gazette, Workers News, The Worker, British Worker and Clarion, each running to hundreds of thousands of copies.*

The ban on the Daily Worker remained in force for nearly 15 months after the nazi invasion of the Soviet Union on 22 June 1941, despite the shift in the Communist Party's view of the war and the alliance of Britain with the Soviet Union. A press statement issued by Rust on 3 July 1941 explains why: "There are quite a number of would-be quislings in high places whose influence is directed against the republication of the Daily Worker, just as they are hostile to a real policy of cooperation with the Soviet Union. Since the banning of the Daily Worker they have enjoyed their immunity from criticism, and their opposition to the lifting of the ban is understandable."

But the campaign against the paper's suppression took on an irresistible momentum. By the end of May 1942, the Labour conference had defied the party's executive to vote for the ban to be lifted. By the time Morrison faced an even bigger reverse at the TUC in September, he had no choice but to concede defeat and the ban was rescinded on 26 August 1942. The Daily Worker reappeared on 7 September, from premises in Swinton Street near King's Cross.

PASS THIS ON TO A FRIEND—

Daily Worker

LATE EDITION

—TEN READERS FOR EVERY COPY!

No. 3431 MONDAY, SEPTEMBER 7, 1942

STALINGRAD BEATS OFF ANOTHER MASS GERMAN ASSAULT

Von Bock's South-West Drive Fails

VON BOCK'S SECOND AND GREATEST MASS ONSLAUGHT AGAINST THE HEROIC CITY OF STALINGRAD HAS BEEN SMASHED AND THE RESISTANCE OF THE DEFENDERS IS STIFFENING, ACCORDING TO A DESPATCH FROM MOSCOW LATE LAST NIGHT.

Though the situation must remain grave while 50 German divisions with thousands of tanks and planes are ceaselessly battering at the gates of the city, the drive from the south-west has failed, **said** Reuter's special correspondent, that was confirmed by the Moscow communique yesterday:—

"All German attempts to break through to the city are meeting with staunch resistance from Soviet troops," it was reported. " During the past 24 hours the Germans have made four attempts on a fortified sector, all of which were unsuccessful.

From JOHN GIBBONS
Daily Worker Special Correspondent

MOSCOW, Sunday night.

THE great Stalingrad battle rages with undiminishing intensity. With first grey stacks of dawn German Junkers and Messerschmitts come over in their hundreds trying by bombing and machine-gunning to pulverise Soviet defences.

Zhukov Presses On West of Moscow

RIVER FORCED

Harry Pollitt's Appeal

I APPEAL on behalf of the Central Committee of the Communist Party to every worker and Party organisation how to save the struggle in the way we all work for the success of the Daily Worker.

How to Win the War

DAILY WORKER'S POLICY

The following declaration of the aims of the Daily Worker has been adopted by the Editorial Board:—

ON this historic day of re-publication the Daily Worker thanks all those in the Labour, trade union, co-operative and democratic movements whose magnificent support not only succeeded in removing the nineteen months' ban, but also very considerably strengthened the unity of the people in the fight for victory over Fascism.

Soviet Tank Unit Struck At Full Speed

From HAROLD KING
Reuter's Special Correspondent

MOSCOW, Sunday night.

Malta Gunners Greet Us

CABLE AND WIRELESS

£50,000

Drive Rommel Back From Our Minefields

ROMMEL'S Africa Corps has been pushed back well off the Egypt battlefront through which they advanced a week ago.

WILLKIE'S TOUR

INDIGESTION GONE IN A FLASH!

RENNIES QUICKLY 'SETTLE ITS HASH'

RENNIES

DIGESTIF

Daily Worker, Monday 29 November 1943

Kiev captives forced to grind bones of burnt comrades

From John Gibbons, Daily Worker Special Correspondent, Kiev, Sunday

In the Hotel Marseilles on Shevchenko Boulevard, Kiev, there is as yet neither light, heat nor water.

Muffled up in a fur hat, overcoat and felt boots, I am writing by flickering candlelight.

Beyond the city, on the plains some fifty miles to the west, big forces of tanks, artillery and infantry are locked in grim and deadly conflict, and the clatter of tanks, guns and motor vehicles heading for the front penetrates through the November gloom with a rumble reminiscent of London's peacetime traffic.

If it is cold and cheerless indoors it is a thousand times more so without. This city, which a bare two years ago ranked as one of the most beautiful in Europe, can only be described now, after seven

---

When the Daily Worker resumed publication, the war had been transformed by the nazi attack on the Soviet Union and the first front page on 7 September reflected that change, with an Editorial Board statement 'How to win the war' and a splash headlined 'Stalingrad beats off another mass German assault.' This was written by the paper's Moscow correspondent John Gibbons, who had worked in Moscow since 1933, first for the Communist International, then as a journalist and broadcaster. He continued to work as a journalist after the war, in Yugoslavia, Romania and Czechoslovakia. He died in 1985.

This despatch, exposing the nazi atrocities at Babi Yar, was one of a series of reports by Gibbons which were subsequently published in a Daily Worker pamphlet, The Most Terrible Place in the World, *a passage from which reads: "It was to this place that the Germans, on*

hundred and seventy-seven days of the fascist "New Order," as the Pompeii of the twentieth century.

Of nearly one million people who lived in Kiev, on the morning of June 22 when the Luftwaffe rained its first bombs on the unsuspecting city, less than ten thousand remained to greet the Red Army when our victorious troops marched through the streets on November 6.

If in Kharkov the German lust for destruction was distinguished by the burning of the city as a whole, in Kiev the burning, thanks to the panicky retreat, was on a slightly lesser scale.

But, and this is the terrible tragedy, the Kiev orgy of mass murder indulged in by the Fascist monsters is without parallel in world history.

The Government Commission now holding an inquiry on the matter of atrocities has not yet presented its findings, but according to its preliminary estimates, over 100,000 people were murdered by the Germans.

From the centre of Kiev on the north-western outskirts of the city, there is an area of waste ground known as Babi Yar. Whenever I speak to people here, the first thing I am asked is: "Have you been to Babi Yar?"

The people of Kiev shudder when they mention this name, and, as Nikolai Bazjhan, deputy chairman of the Council of People's Commissars of the Ukrainian Republic, said to me, "There is no more terrible place on earth than Babi Yar."

Later, when our group of foreign correspondents visited Babi Yar, what I saw there soon convinced me of the awful truth of Bazjhan's words.

September 22, 1941, drove the entire Jewish population of Kiev, numbering 60,000 people. Plank platforms were spaced at intervals across the pits, and on these the aged and infirm, women and children were placed in batches. Men then sprayed the platforms with machine-gun fire and the victims toppled into the pits. Many were only wounded by the bullets, but were buried alive by the monsters supervising the slaughter. This went on for three days, and by the evening of the third day the Jewish population of Kiev, with the exception of a few families concealed by neighbours, had ceased to exist."

Three hundred prisoners were taken to this place. With their legs manacled, working under the eyes of SS Guards posted all round the sandpits, they were forced to dig up bodies of people who had been massacred there in preparation for burning.

A nearby Jewish cemetery was depleted of tombstones and grave railings which were used for the purpose of building nearly a hundred improvised "furnaces."

Every day for seven weeks the three hundred prisoners were compelled to dig up decomposed and decomposing bodies and drag them to the furnaces. Arms, legs and heads often came asunder. The sandpits are still littered with human remains.

Oil was poured over the bodies, which were piled up twenty feet high with a layer of firewood between each row. Preparations for the burning of a hundred or so furnaces went on during the day, and at night time they were fired, with relays of prisoners forced to work as "stokers."

In the early mornings the smoke from these pyres was clearly visible in Kiev and although the approaches to the scene of this ghoulish work were carefully guarded by SS troops, the acrid smell of burning flesh told the people of Kiev what was happening.

Three hundred Red Army prisoners lived in dugouts deprived of all contact with their fellow-prisoners.

Some were given the job of pounding charred bones to bits, while others were given the job of sifting ashes for rings, earrings, and gold teeth, etc. After each burning ashes and dust from the pounded bones were carefully scattered over the waste ground.

Toward the end of September, when this most frightful of jobs was nearing completion, the prisoners who anticipated being shot and burned began to plan their escape. House keys found on the clothes of slaughtered people were manipulated by fitters and locksmiths among them, and on the night of September 28 the survivors of the original three hundred opened their doors and, helped by others, managed to file their shackles before being observed by SS sentries.

Upon discovery the men began to run. A dozen machine-guns sent a stream of bullets in all directions, and of more than two hundred men only twelve made their escape from Babi Yar, the remainder were cut down.

Of the twelve, seven are now in Kiev working with the Government Commission, and right there in the sandpits, three of them, Lieuts Ostrov and Davidov, and Regimental Quartermaster Vilkis related details of the Babi Yar massacre, and the disposal of the bodies.

I know that there are people who find it hard to believe that the Germans are capable of such horrible crimes.

But there in the sandpits of Babi Yar with pieces of bodies all around, 16 newspapermen from Britain and America questioned, and requestioned, and questioned again three Red Army men who were forced to take part in the work.

Each time the answers came clear and direct without a moment's hesitation, without the slightest contradiction. Men even pulled up their trousers and showed us the still festering wounds caused by the iron rings with which their legs were shackled.

Charred stonework and tombstones used for the furnaces were still lying there in the sand.

The chimes of history

By Ilya Ehrenburg

The measure of time is relative – but each time we are deeply stirred on the eve of the New Year as if an invisible line separated one hour from the next. Involuntarily we look back. The snowstorm has not yet covered up the traces of sorrow and suffering.

Only a year ago the Germans were in the Crimea and the suburbs of Leningrad. Russia has forced rivers, crossed mountains. But it is not of conquests she is thinking. For the Russian war is sorrow, sacrifice, baseness – never a profession.

We do not want to force upon anybody our ideas, orders and customs. Now everybody talks about freedom. It is the readiest word. Well, people conceive "freedom" in different ways. There are different ways of breathing; but one thing is beyond doubt – if a man cannot breathe, he must die.

The approach of the Red Army is changing the world. Prisons are opening, tongues are loosed. People utter stirring words, curse and bless, cry and laugh. They have returned to life.

Those malevolent toward us maintain that we want to bring on bayonets that very freedom which our people found in October, which they gained in suffering, in 25 years of privation, toil, struggle and solitude.

Bayonets cannot create free people, they can merely destroy jailers.

Why do the anti-Fascists of a Fascist kind so much fear our victories? Probably because we do not replace the fetters of one sort with others.

The renowned Soviet author Ilya Ehrenburg acted as a war correspondent for the Red Army newspaper Red Star. His articles and broadcasts, which played an outstanding role in rallying the Soviet armed forces and wider population against the nazis, were regularly reprinted in the Daily Worker.

We do not disarm the Slovak patriots. We do not demand that the Yugoslavs subordinate themselves to Mihailovich. We do not force the Norwegians to seek reconciliation with their quislings. How people wish to live – that is their own affair. The Red Army is busy with its own job. It is removing the hangmen.

The Red Army has crossed the frontiers as an army of liberation.

If Paris is ruled not by the Germans or the Petains, nor by the half-Germans or the half-Petains who were ready to seize France in the Algiers period, this is explained to a certain extent by the victories of the Red Army.

If Yugoslavia has not suffered the fate of her neighbouring countries; if the Bulgarian people is trying its traitors; if there are ten parties and a hundred factions in Lublin who were persecuted under Pilsudski and who are now able to argue freely about the future of Poland – then therein lies the service rendered by the Red Army.

An old French book writes about a certain Jean the Beekeeper. Possessing great strength, he was kind-hearted and did not interfere in the affairs of even his close neighbours; but for 100 leagues around people said it was dangerous to offend an orphan or hide a dishonest man because Jean the Beekeeper might hear of it.

His very existence alone froze the hearts of miscreants and inspired the worthy. Victims frequently stopped offenders with the words: "Jean the Beekeeper will learn of this."

Word of the Red Army goes not a hundred but a thousand leagues. And though the commandant of some Hungarian town, a captain from Penza, says: "We do not interfere in your affairs," yet much changes in that town, and the prisons open twice – once to let out the free, and again to take in the traitors.

Over immeasurable distance the steps of the Volga farmers and the Urals workers can be heard. Even in distant Spain the people has half-raised its head. It knows that there is a Jean the Beekeeper in the world.

The everyday casts a veil over history, but at New Year, through that spiritual attunement which gives birth to feeling, let us have a look at what has happened.

Not merely a series of brilliant victories; not merely the storming of one fortress after another, the forcing of one river or another, not merely the clearing of our territory or the liberation of many countries – but something more.

The Red Army has saved civilisation.

Today it is clear to everyone that the victory of fascism would have been the end of civilisation.

Perhaps after Hitler's victory, towns, museums, gardens would have survived, but Fascism destroys the essence of man, the thinking man, and would thus have destroyed architects, and poets and gardeners. In several generations the world, gone savage, would have begun to look like the Rome of the Barbarians.

The Red Army saved mankind from this. And no greetings, no presentations or addresses can express what the world owes to Stalingrad. It is better in this case either to be silent or to say what a young French girl said when being led out to be shot by the Germans: "Friends, there is Russia!"

It was not within our power to save the world from war. Among the defenders of culture there were blind men and hypocrites. In the West they repeated the word "peace" while dreaming of war in the East.

We were unable to save the world from war – but we have saved it from perishing. Without Soviet consciousness and Russian steadfastness there would have been neither liberty nor culture today – and various foreign Pharisees would not be able to discuss how to protect from inevitable retribution those who worked for Himmler.

The blood of Russia saved the world. And, thinking over the significance of what has happened, we see that by our side stand ghosts dear to us.

Let no one say that we have forgotten them. Perhaps it would be easier if we could forget, but the heart is not made like that. Under the ashes of the years are the red coals of remembrance.

I want to speak of those who perished without having seen even the dawn of victory, of those who battled in the most terrible days, whom no one saluted since those battles were lost – but without those lost battles there would not have been victory.

I want to speak of those who fell during the retreat, when whole regiments died so as to give the Motherland a day and sometimes an hour; of those who died in unsuccessful assaults, as when people died at Rzhev for Stalingrad.

Who has not someone near and dear – a brother, a son or friend – among these ghosts? Let the years smooth down the humps of the graves. Let sun and rain rub off the names on the little boards. Marble is stronger, but even marble crumbles.

Their immortality lies elsewhere – in the immortality of the cause for which they died. And we, their near and dear ones, we of their age, their friends and brothers in arms – we shall not forget them to our very last hour.

Those dead are with us. Their battalions, their regiments and their divisions storm enemy towns with us. They warm themselves with us at the dim bonfires. They sigh bitterly with us as we write on the flap of the envelope: "I have survived and am happy." They will come with us to Berlin.

And of this we think as we look into the New Year – of our old friends, those who did not betray and whom we will not betray.

We are approaching our goal. I do not envy the Germans. All they have is in the past, and about them the ruins of cities. Rumours and sirens – sirens and rumours.

The death which they carried to the world has returned to them like a boomerang. In vain do the Germans count on other people's stupidity. They think that if they can hold up the judges on the threshold of the court the judges will stop, grumble a little, and disperse.

The Germans do not know what forces they have awakened. Those who have seen the furnaces of Maidenek will seek out the stokers. We have lived through too much not to visit Berlin.

We have not betrayed ourselves. As before, we believe in brotherhood; and if the Germans have excluded themselves from the universal family it is not our ideas which are at fault, but the crimes of the Germans.

To them we promise neither sympathy nor leniency. We shall try to see that 1945 is Germany's last year.

To the peoples we offer our friendship. We have lived through not a little and today even young people have grey hairs. We shall understand one another.

Diplomats are fond of saying that they sit at round tables, though these round tables have sharp corners. But the table of the peoples is truly round. On it we shall cut the first bread of peace and pour out the wine of liberty.

What makes our Commander-in-Chief strong and famed is that he knows the taste of this bread and the aroma of this wine. His name is being repeated today as the name of a friend by people infinitely far from our country. He is thought of with hope. The peoples, wishing him health, thus wish themselves happiness and peace.

Hark, friends! The chimes of history are striking. We are beginning not a fresh page but fresh annals. It is dangerous to forecast, and not really necessary. But the heart and mind repeat that the year of 1945 will be the first year of another, great life – the life for which we have suffered.

Daily Worker, Saturday 6 December 1947

The Savoy strike scandal

George Sinfield

The so-called settlement of the Savoy strike is the worst of its kind in recent industrial history.

The indifference, the almost callous indifference, of some National Union of General and Municipal Workers officials to their elementary duty of defending members struggling to uphold the first principle of trade unionism, has shocked the labour movement.

This folly may cause grave damage to organisation among catering workers, many of whom, though babes in experience, are giants in desire to be organised.

For four weeks over 800 strikers, of various races and creeds, of many 'isms and none at all, fought to establish a right won by other workers many decades ago.

They expected their executive committee, who are paid for the job, to fight with them to the bitter end.

Capitulation was the last thing they had in mind. Now they say their aspirations were cruel dreams: that the executive committee is completely out of touch with the membership.

The Daily Worker's slogan on the eve of the 1945 general election was "vote as red as you can". But the first majority Labour government was to show itself stained deepest red in the blood that never dries of British imperialism. At home, too, despite the gains of the welfare state and nationalisation, the right wing maintained its grip, as the episode of the Savoy strike illustrates.

George Sinfield had begun with the Daily Worker before the war covering sports, reflecting his long involvement the workers' sports movement. But his main contribution was as the paper's industrial correspondent, a role which he fulfilled until his retirement in 1967. A collection of Sinfield's memoirs, His Pen A Sword, *was edited after his death in 1973.*

The committee are to inquire into the strike and that popular leader Arthur Lewis may be on the carpet.

In all sincerity I here state that hundreds of members would regard "disciplinary" action against Lewis as a further insult.

Mr Lewis, together with Frank Piazza, the waiter around whom the dispute took place, and Jim Blair, branch representative on the London District Committee of the union, were prevented by the executive committee from attending the meeting called to explain the terms of the settlement.

I watched the faces of the strikers as they left that meeting. They were the faces of disillusioned men and women.

Not one, but dozens, spoke of "sell-out" and "carve-up." They felt deserted and humiliated.

Scores said they would "tear up their cards."

Executive committee members present knew this, but appeared to care little, and even less for the impression gained by the reporters present.

The public expected a full statement from the executive committee concerning the meeting. But it was not given.

One had to extract information from Harold Crane, the union's industrial officer, and that, I submit, is striking commentary on the lamentable conception of responsibility to the public, particularly to trade unionists who form such a large part of it.

Engineers, miners, dockers, market workers, railwaymen and, indeed, all organised workers will ask what sort of mentality motivated the executive committee to conclude an agreement which has all the appearance of being dictated by the Savoy.

Piazza is to be found work elsewhere and the rest of the workers – waitresses and cooks, platemen and porters – many of whom have suffered badgering and pushing around by the police, now find they may be victimised.

Seventy-five per cent are to be reinstated in two weeks and the remainder re-engaged when "the opportunity affords."

No worse settlement has been concluded since the fateful days of the 1926 General Strike, when the majority of the workers, who had struck in sympathy with the mineworkers, were left to get back to work in the best way they could.

Make no mistake about this: the organised workers' movement will be astounded at the incredible manner the NUGMW executive committee ended this strike.

Union secretary Tom Williamson MP is reported to have told the strikers several weeks ago that any proposed settlement would first be put to the workers.

But what, in fact, happened? The agreement, settled in the sumptuous sanctum of the Savoy, was presented to the workers as an accomplished fact.

The strikers had to lump it or leave it.

These discarded men and women of the Savoy were not miners or railwaymen, or other workers engaged on vital production. They work so that privileged people can guzzle and gorge in splendid surroundings.

But they were fighting for a cherished principle of proper trade union recognition, for a decent living, and in that sense are as important as workers in other industries.

And it was they, remember, who felt the fury of police interference, backed up, it is regrettable to say, by a Labour Home Secretary.

This police action was taken at a decisive point in the dispute when the pickets were holding up the delivery of oil to the hotels. It must be recorded as an official act of hostility to the workers' struggle at a moment when a friendly gesture from the government would have meant victory for the strikers.

The strikers likewise witnessed the refusal of the employers to accept the findings of a joint committee of inquiry calling for the reinstatement of Mr Piazza – allegedly guilty of an indiscretion – after 14 days' suspension.

They saw this refusal insolently maintained when the management defied the Labour Ministry's arbitration tribunal which, after a full investigation, endorsed the committee's decision.

And all this time the workers have tried to end the paralysis of their own leaders who stood back apparently in fear of the Savoy management.

What other indignity must the workers suffer in the fight for trade union recognition and that Labour may continue to rule?

Workers who see the building of unity as their first duty will support any sound move within the NUGMW to strengthen the leadership so that it may lead from the front – and not totter along behind: and work in the interests of members and not, as hundreds of strikers say, in the interests of the employers.

I have heard numbers declare that catering workers should be organised in their own trade union and that the NUGMW is too much of an octopus to do the job properly.

That, of course, is for catering workers themselves to decide: and the first move was taken last Thursday when one branch called on the TUC to help in this direction.

Finally, trade unionists will watch with closest attention the future of Arthur Lewis in the union. Rumours are rife that a section of the leadership is out to remove this courageous Labour MP.

Any such move would be the last straw. Mr Lewis has done more for catering workers in nine minutes than the rest of the leaders have in nine years.

He has stumped the country and suffered insult and arrest for a cause that is just.

Action against him would make even blacker the scandal of the Savoy. It must not happen.

It is to be sincerely hoped that when the strikers have revived after the first shock of the shabby treatment they have received from their own executive committee they will realise the futility of tearing up their union cards.

That would be a defeatist act and play into the hands of those who might be glad to see them leave the union.

Rather the kick they have had should kindle the spark of determination to change the policy of the union and to elect leaders capable of truly representing their interests.

Daily Worker, Tuesday 14 December 1948

The landlords' sacred bird

Wilfred Willett

The sunbeams slant over the field to the western edge of the wood, heightening with soft gold the many colours of tree and coppice.

Cock pheasants walk sedately about the field near the wood, picking up insects and seeds like barnyard fowls.

The glory of their plumage shines forth, more brilliant than any other British bird's, with the lovely browns and gold of the body feathers flecked with dark bars to the end of the long, graduated tail.

The head is green with red wattles surrounding the eyes, and very often since the introduction of Chinese birds, who have hybridised the original stock, there is a white neck ring.

Among the cocks are hens, in their less conspicuous grey-brown plumage.

The pheasant is a native of China, Mongolia, and indeed, throughout Asia, and even as far west as Bulgaria.

It seems, here at least, to have no migratory instincts and stays around where it was hatched.

Some people think that the Romans must have introduced it into this country, for there are records of the bird in old account books before the Battle of Hastings.

It seems likely that the practical Romans should have introduced this easily trapped bird, that would fatten on the acorns and other wild food, and so give the Roman officers a tasty roast for festive banquets.

Wilfred Willett contributed the Nature Notebook to the Daily Worker for many years – his first signed piece, 'The Countryside and the People', appeared in April 1938. His book, British Birds, *was published in the 1940s. Willett combined his interests with efforts to organise rural workers. He was badly wounded in the First World War and his personal story was dramatised for television in the early 1980s.*

After the Roman occupation ended, pheasants roamed the forests' edges where they joined the common fields, but probably it was a rare bird till the end of the 18th Century.

For although it was classed as "game," until the introduction of the fowling-piece the nobility would hardly prize the cover-skulking pheasant as suitable quarry for their hawks.

After the English Revolution, the new ruling class soon began to increase its wealth by developing new forms of production. Shooting became a craze.

In 1770, new Game Laws were enacted which were class legislation with vengeance and violence.

In 1785 the Chinese ring-necked pheasant was first introduced to add to our native stock and woods began to be reserved for pheasants.

Great enclosures of the common land and woods began and in 50 years over three million acres were taken without any payment, and much more at only a tithe of its value.

The dispossessed peasants who had gathered sticks and their fuel in the woods found their ancient right taken from them.

In the woods, with the increasing number of pheasants, were spring guns, which were fired by a trip-cord and killed without warning, and steel man-traps which caught men like rabbits.

All through the 19th Century the wages paid to farm workers were such that they had either to starve or poach. Cobbett tells of a young man cracking stones on the roadside, who on being asked how he lived on half-a-crown a week replied:

"I don't. I poach; it is better to be hanged than starved to death."

Men and children were hanged, transported for life, or imprisoned. Village gangs – desperate with hunger – raided the woods to get something to feed their starving families on, and fights with keepers in which some one would be killed were common.

In no country has a law been so unmercifully applied against the people as the English Game Laws by the landed gentry.

W H Hudson writes in "A Shepherd's Life":

"Judges in their summings up and sentences... the awful power they possessed, and its constant exercise, had not only produced the inevitable hardening effect, but had made them cruel in the true sense of the word. Their pleasure in passing dreadful sentences was very thinly disguised by certain lofty phrases as to the necessity of upholding the law, morality and religion."

And this happened in living memory. Yet village folk have always looked down on one who was a "professional" poacher.

I have seen many bushels of corn strewn every day in the woods for pheasants when many farmworkers could not get work or enough food.

And later the golden birds were scared out of the woods and slaughtered in hundreds by the landowning nobility who did not even load their own guns.

Now I can never watch this lovely woodland bird without being reminded of some of the fiercest class struggles in English history – no, not even when I see them hanging in poulterers' shops with Christmas greetings about brotherhood all around.

Is Britain imperialist?

R Palme Dutt

Listeners to Itma will have heard Tommy Handley the other week trying Twenty Questions. "The object I have thought of is the British Empire."

"Fact or fiction?" "Fiction."

Mr Attlee must have been taking lessons from Tommy Handley when he made his recent speech at the Lord Mayor's banquet, objecting to Soviet criticism of "members of His Majesty's Government as imperialists," and referred in disproof to "self-government in India, Burma and Malta":

"It is surely strange that in face of these facts Russian statesmen and journalists will accuse Britain of imperialism. If there is imperialism in the world today, by which I mean the subjection of other peoples by the political and economic domination of a powerful nation, it is certainly not to be found in the British Commonwealth."

Mr Attlee was speaking in the historic Mansion House to an audience of City magnates whose wealth is built on colonial plunder, where even the traditional gold plate of the classic banquet is drawn from the agony of African slavery (the South African gold mine workers get 2s 5d a day, to yield £43 million profits, and when they dared to strike last year were batoned back into the mines, with numbers killed and hundreds arrested).

When he stepped out of the Mansion House, glowing with conscious virtue, he stepped into the midst of the imposing edifices of the great monopolies whose very names cry Empire exploitation –

R Palme Dutt was one of the leading theoreticians of the Communist Party throughout its first four decades, becoming general secretary after the outbreak of the Second World War until the summer of 1941. Palme Dutt, the editor of Labour Monthly, also edited the Daily Worker between the years 1936 and 1938 and regularly contributed articles.

Anglo-Iranian Oil Company, Imperial Tobacco, Royal Dutch Shell, Unilevers, Consolidated Goldfields.

But, of course, British imperialism does not exist. It is only a dream of suspicious Russians.

This grand new fairy-tale about the Empire that isn't there is nowadays so assiduously repeated by His Majesty's Ministers, docile journalists on the News Chronicle and Daily Herald, Tory Colonial Governors lecturing on the BBC, and similar authorities, that simpler members of the Labour movement have almost begun to believe it.

Oddly enough there are two entirely opposite viewpoints which Government Ministers love to present about the Empire today – and the same Ministers present both.

At one time they tell us, like Mr Attlee, that there is really no such thing as British imperialism. Charges of "imperialism" are declared to be "obsolete" and "out of date."

Mr Morrison proclaimed in September, 1946: "We need not be unduly concerned if people seek to attach to us obsolete labels such as 'imperialism' and 'capitalism'."

But the next moment the same Ministers are proclaiming their passionate devotion to the existing Empire in the best Tory fashion, and declaring it to the indispensable foundation for the prosperity of the British working class.

The same Mr Morrison announced in January, 1946: "We are great friends of the jolly old Empire and are going to stick to it."

And Mr Bevin is especially fond of lecturing on the theme that the Empire interests of British capitalism are of vital importance for the wage packets of British workers.

Why this contradiction? Which is the real voice? The contradiction lies in the facts.

British imperialism once held an unchallenged world monopoly. Out of the profits of this monopoly it could give crumbs to a privileged minority of the workers.

This is the basis of the old traditional Labour imperialism, which is most clearly expressed today by Bevin. But this old basis is today breaking down.

United States imperialism has taken over the dominant world position from Britain.

Over large areas British imperialism has to retreat, to surrender here to the United States (in the Far East), there to the national movements (in India and Burma), to manoeuvre, to seek to maintain indirect control.

Over other areas British imperialism seeks to maintain hold by armed force. But even this throws crippling burdens on the weakened British economy.

For purposes of propaganda, all the limelight is turned on the areas where the strength of the national movement has compelled a retreat, but under cover of this propaganda the people are called on to make sacrifices and support colossal armed forces in order to maintain a grip on the remaining areas.

Troops may be withdrawn from Palestine – to be concentrated in Irak or Transjordan. They may be removed from Alexandria – to be concentrated in the Canal Zone.

A new base is prepared in East Africa. Ceylon is granted a species of "self-government" – subject to maintenance of the naval base of Trincomalee. New air bases are being developed in India.

Indian "independence" is tempered by partition and the independence of the princes.

Burma may be granted "independence"; but a British Military Mission is to remain, the resources of the country belong to the overseas monopolies, and a crushing burden of debt is imposed. Troops may be withdrawn from Burma; but 35,000 troops are maintained in Malaya.

This is the politics and strategy of imperialism in decline.

Even while the ground begins to grow too hot in the Middle East, new schemes of Empire concentration and exploitation are intensified in the last stronghold – Africa.

The Royal Tour to South Africa was the signal of the new orientation. British capital migrates to South Africa, Rhodesia, East Africa.

The Colonial Development Corporation is announced, with £100,000,000 capital; the Overseas Food Corporation, with £50,000,000; the East Africa Ground Nuts Scheme, with £24,000,000.

These schemes are also presented as a "Socialist colonial policy." In fact, they bear all the old marks.

They are to be operated through the great monopolies. The Ground

Nuts Scheme was devised by Unilevers, and is to be operated by the United Africa Co, a subsidiary of Unilevers.

The Colonial Development Corporation is to "operate on commercial principles"; "it is not intended to supplant private enterprise, but to supplement it." (Creech Jones in Parliament, June 25).

Huge plantations with plantation labour at colonial rates of wages are to be organised.

In place of industrialisation and balanced economic development the old vicious colonial system of mono-culture is to be extended; the colonies are to be exploited as agricultural reserves of the imperialist metropolis.

This is indeed not "socialism." It is the new streamlined imperialism.

The final test does not lie only in the field of Colonial exploitation, but in the realm of world politics.

In the present world alignment of two camps, the Imperialist Camp and the Democratic Camp, where does Britain stand?

There is no question of the progressive democratic sentiments of the overwhelming majority of the people, of their sympathies for Socialism, the Soviet Union and the new democracies.

But in the hard facts of world politics today, Britain, under the present Right-Wing Labour Government, is lined up in the Imperialist Camp, operating in opposition to the Soviet Union and the new democracies.

Britain votes with imperialist reaction in the United Nations. British troops, linked with American dollars, are used to back reaction and for imperialist policing in many areas of the world – glaringly in Greece.

This policy is costing Britain dear and is the root cause of Britain's crisis. We must change it.

We need not lament the decline of the old Empire. It brought profits for the few; but it brought misery for the colonial peoples; and for the British people it brought neglect of home industry and agriculture, derelict areas and mass unemployment and war.

That old basis is bankrupt. In our present crisis we are paying the price of Empire.

A new era must open.

Daily Worker, Monday 28 April 1952

This is the war in Malaya

By The Editor

The accompanying picture reveals, better than a million words could do the bestial character of the war now being waged in Malaya.

Though waged in the name of the British people, this war is a blot on the national honour and is a deadly blow at the true interests of the British people.

The picture, taken by a British soldier, shows a British Marine Commando and members of the British puppet forces in Malaya,

The exposure by the Daily Worker of the barbaric practice of head-hunting in the war against the Malayan liberation forces was directed against a Conservative government. However, as the Gabriel cartoon from August 1948 makes clear, the policy had been initiated years before under the Labour government of Clement Attlee. The cartoon was drawn following the Daily Worker's splash on 12 August,

sporting with the severed head of a member of the Malayan liberation forces.

More awful than the sadistic "sport" in the foreground is that British troops are seen going about their ordinary business.

Neither officer nor man intervenes to stop the self-degradation of the group of men concerned.

There can be no doubt as to the authenticity of the picture, taken by a British soldier in the area of Kuala Kesan, in the second half of last year.

The photograph illuminates a further descent into bestiality.

The collective punishment of whole villages, the destruction of crops from the air, is accompanied by degrading "fun" with the severed heads of Malayan patriots.

Those who wage unjust wars against colonial peoples inevitably dehumanise themselves.

For in such wars the "enemy" is the whole people, resolutely determined to be free.

Strategy, tactics and technical superiority, which might be used against a compact army in the field are paralysed when it is a matter of fighting a whole people.

The only alternatives are to give the people the national independence it desires, or to sink into ever fouler depths of degradation by the employment of methods which are designed to cow an entire population into submission.

Those methods will fail in the long run. Meanwhile, they degrade those who order them and those who execute them.

They blacken the name of the British people before the whole civilised world.

'Head-hunters are flown to fight Malay democrats,' which revealed: "The British government is recruiting Dyaks – savage head-hunters from Sarawak – to track down members of the outlawed popular movement in the Malayan jungle."

The Daily Worker's editor was by now John Ross Campbell, who had taken over following the death of William Rust in February 1949, having previously edited the paper briefly in 1939 and acted as assistant editor since 1942.

In Geneva in 1949 the British Government signed the revised Geneva Conventions which dealt, among other things, with colonial wars.

Look at this picture and see how these conventions are being carried out.

All these bestialities are to protect the profits of the tin and rubber companies.

Britain does not require to occupy and oppress Malaya in order to get rubber and tin.

It could, by honest trade, get all the tin and rubber it requires from an independent Malaya.

It is the profits of the few that are being safeguarded in Malaya and nothing else.

The British people should firmly resolve that they not allow their sons to be killed and de-civilised for this purpose.

They should force the British Government to grant independence to Malaya, withdraw its troops and seek to arrive at a new and just form of co-operation with the independent Malayan Government and peoples.

That is the way of honour and national interest. The one which we are treading now leads to defeat, shame and national betrayal.

This picture was taken by a young British soldier just back from Malaya.

The severed head belonged to a Malayan patriot, shot during a jungle patrol. "It was not," said the soldier, "an uncommon experience."

It happened late last year in the village of Kuala Kesan (known to troops as K.K.)

Standing beside a Royal Marine Commando are two Asian soldiers recruited by the British, one of whom wears a crucifix. Other Commandos can be seen behind.

In the background is a hut with the sign: "40 Commando R.M."

Since the picture was taken, a fine of 200 Straits dollars (£23 6s) has been imposed on anybody taking photographs.

The soldier who took this photograph said: "We can never win in Malaya. The guerillas are too well organised. The people are with them. The morale of our lads is low."

He added that American officers have been going out with British patrols for "experience."

Daily Worker Wednesday April 30 1952

These are no fakes

From Frank Gullett, News Editor

The Admiralty is trying to cast doubt on the authenticity of the Malaya horror picture published in the Daily Worker on Monday.

The photograph showed a British Commando with an Asian soldier holding up the severed head of a Malayan patriot killed during a jungle patrol.

National and provincial newspapers yesterday printed inspired stories quoting an Admiralty spokesman who hinted that the picture was a "fake."

We are prepared to take up this "fake" challenge. Much as we dislike printing photographs of this nature we here reproduce another from the same source. Others are in our possession. The Asian soldier appearing in this picture is the same one as in Monday's reproduction. He wears a crucifix.

In the background are British Commandos outside an army hut with the signs: 40 Commando RM; Heavy Weapons Group Office; MMG Section; Sniper Section; 3rd Mortar Section.

Today in the House of Commons a further attempt may be made to insinuate that the pictures are faked. Colonel Crossthwaite-Eyre (Con, New Forest) will ask the First Lord of the Admiralty, Mr J.P.L. Thomas, for a statement during question time.

His query is framed in indirect form and it asks Mr Thomas "if he will make a statement on the recent engagements in which the Royal Marines have been concerned in Malaya."

After his main question has been answered, it is expected he will ask a supplementary question about the picture and call on Mr Thomas to say whether he believes it to be genuine.

Yesterday, an Admiralty spokesman, referring to the picture in

Monday's paper, said: "To Admiralty minds the picture is a fake." What are the "Admiralty minds?"

Asked if the picture had been submitted to photographic experts, the spokesman said: "I'm afraid I cannot say."

Inquiries are now being made in Malaya. How long will these inquiries take? The spokesman thought they would be "somewhat prolonged."

For the benefit of the Admiralty, Tory MPs and those who doubt that such things could possibly happen in war-torn Malaya, here are the facts about the pictures.

They were taken by a young British soldier who has just returned to this country after service in Malaya. The events took place last year in the village of Kuala Kesan (known to troops as K.K.).

The soldier in question – we are withholding his name, number and unit – was interviewed by a staff reporter and gave full details, and others too gruesome to publish, of what was happening in Malaya when these pictures were taken.

British Army officers cannot be ignorant of what was taking place. Since these pictures were taken a fine of 200 Straits dollars (£23 6s) has been imposed on anybody taking similar photographs.

The pictures we reproduce were initially contact prints from a $2^1/_4$in by $3^1/_4$in negative. This is the most popular size with amateur photographers, and usually the one camera soldiers overseas employ.

Daily Worker Thursday May 8 1952

Govt. admits Malaya atrocity

From Malcolm MacEwen

It was officially admitted in the House of Commons yesterday that photographs published of the severed head of a Malayan Liberation fighter, taken at a Marine Commando unit, are genuine.

This admission was drawn from Mr Oliver Lyttelton, the Colonial Secretary, by Mr Emrys Hughes (Lab, S Ayrshire), who asked: "Does Mr Lyttelton say this was a genuine photograph and is he definitely convinced it was not a fake?"

Mr Lyttelton replied: "Yes, it is a genuine photograph."

The Colonial Secretary had been asked by Mr Awbery (Lab, Central Bristol) if he would make a statement "about the severing of heads of 'bandits' in Malaya."

Mr Lyttelton said: "The incident which gave rise to the photograph which has appeared in the Daily Worker occurred in April 1951 when a jungle patrol was ambushed by bandits.

"The officer and corporal were killed, and two other members of the patrol badly wounded. One bandit was shot dead.

"After the bandits had retired a tribesman, not a Royal Marine, who had acted as a tracker, decapitated the body.

"The head was brought in for identification. The photograph was not authorised and should not have been taken.

"Instructions have been given to the High Commissioner that bodies should not be decapitated for identification, which should be secured by photographs and fingerprints."

Mr Awbery said nearly all members on his side of the House were agreed that such methods as were suggested in the photograph were not desirable.

He asked Mr Lyttelton to give definite instructions in the future that such gruesome methods would not be adopted even in jungle warfare.

Mr Lyttelton replied: "I have already in my answer explained that decapitation is not to take place.

"I am afraid I shall be in some difficulty in explaining what happened in April 1951."

'Shall we send it to Mr. Attlee with our Progress Report?'

Daily Worker, Thursday 10 August 1950

US Belsen in Korea

Alan Winnington, our special correspondent with the Korean People's Army, has sent the following cable from the village of Rang Wul, near Taejon. It appeared in the later editions of the Daily Worker yesterday

Seven thousand people have been horribly butchered in a little valley about one kilometre from this village under the supervision of American officers.

American service rifle, pistol and carbine bullets were used to kill them. The trucks that drove them to their deaths were American, and some of the drivers were American.

The 40 cigarette packets which still litter the scene are American. The shooting, beating and beheading were done by South Korean puppet police, but this is an American crime – one of the worst the world has ever known.

Great ditches like those at Belsen and Buchenwald were used to try to hide the traces of the massacre.

I have spent the last few days in ascertaining a whole series of such American atrocities carried out under the instructions of American

Alan Winnington joined the Daily Worker in 1942, when staff had to be found and trained rapidly after the ban was lifted. He had previously worked as press officer for the Communist Party. Allen Hutt, the paper's chief sub-editor, trained him to become his deputy "in two terrible and almost sleepless weeks", according to Winnington's memoirs, Breakfast With Mao, *and he shared the chief-subbing duties with Hutt for the next six years.*

In 1948, Winnington was sent to China and entered Beijing alongside the victorious leaders of the Chinese Communist Party in early 1949. But it was for his reports as special correspondent with the Korean People's Army – exposing atrocities carried out by the US and South Korean forces, and the manoeuvres later employed by the US to stall the ceasefire talks – that he became best known.

"advisers." In view of the evidence only one conclusion is possible: what has happened here is the same as happened in Europe.

As soon as the Syngman Rhee-Truman conspiracy to invade the North was launched, orders were given for the systematic physical annihilation of all political prisoners then in Syngman Rhee's jails.

The number was between 200,000 and 400,000, but will never exactly be known.

Rang Wul village lies seven kilometres south-east of Taejon on the main road.

I have spent many hours here, yesterday and today, visiting the death pits taking photographs, collecting a few of the thousands of American cartridge cases that litter the ground, interrogating more than 20 eye-witnesses separately, and checking evidence. Here is the story:

On July 2, truckloads of Rhee's police rode into the village and mobilised the villagers and others from nearby places at rifle point to go into the valley and dig a series of great pits.

There were six of them, the largest being 200 yards long, varying between four and two yards wide, and of a uniform depth of two yards.

As soon as the first pit was ready on July 4, police began to bring prisoners from the local jails to the spot in American trucks.

The method of packing the prisoners on the trucks was as follows:

This report, and similar material published in October 1950 as a Daily Worker pamphlet by Winnington, I Saw The Truth In Korea, led to discussions in the Labour Cabinet, which endorsed the allegation first raised by the Attorney General Sir Hartley Shawcross that the pamphlet constituted 'treason', a charge carrying the death penalty.

But the Cabinet was unwilling to prosecute, fearing that a jury would refuse to convict. Ministers were also mindful of the fate of a previous government, which had attempted to level charges against the editor, John Ross Campbell, who, in 1924, had been charged with sedition while acting editor of the Workers Weekly, one of the forerunners of the Daily Worker. The episode precipitated the fall of the first Labour government when the case was dropped.

Winnington recalled in an article for the Morning Star in January

at the jails they were beaten unconscious with heavy sticks and piled into the trucks, first a layer of men, then one of women, then another layer of men, and so on, like sardines.

On top sat the police. Each truckload contained more than 50 prisoners, every one having his or her hands tied with wire behind them.

Just before the trucks reached the valley two American jeeps arrived with high officers of the American and puppet armies, who stood around smoking and chatting.

The trucks were driven to the side of the first pit and the prisoners flung out. Some of them in the bottom layer appeared already dead, most were half-conscious from the beatings, and because they had been starved for three days.

Those capable of maintaining a kneeling position were forced down and given a volley of six or so shots from behind. This was the case at first.

Later, after the second truckload, an American officer was seen to be arguing with the puppet officers, making signs with his fingers and shaking his head.

After that, each prisoner got one bullet in the chest or back of the neck and if this failed to kill a Japanese sword was used to do the rest.

Those incapable of kneeling were shot on the ground or killed with a sweep of the sword.

1981, headlined 'I would do it again': "The first words of a pamphlet for which Sir Hartley Shawcross considered hanging a few of us read: 'In the mountains of Korea, the sons of British mothers lie rotting in the wind.' Tokens of Whitehall's subservience to Truman." He remained as forthright in defence of his exposures of the US use of napalm and germ warfare in Korea.

Winnington paid the price when, at the end of the war, the British government refused to renew his passport, effectively exiling him. It was some 20 years before he was able to visit Britain again. He worked as a correspondent for the Daily Worker and Morning Star, first in China and then, from the early 1960s, Berlin. He died in 1983.

Winnington's brother, Richard, was a noted film critic for the News Chronicle and contributed reviews to the Daily Worker during the 1940s under the pseudonym 'John Ross' (from John Ross Campbell).

The bodies were bundled into the pits. As each section was filled the peasants were made to throw in a layer of soil and stamp it down while the trucks moved on to a new section.

The first series of massacres went on for three days, July 4, 5 and 6.

Daily Worker, Tuesday 20 May 1952

The most terrible Korea story

Alan Winnington, Kaesong, Monday

There are many victims of napalm in this town, mostly women and children, because most of its victims are women and children.

Many of them are so conscious of their disfigurements that they refuse to be interviewed or photographed.

A boy who was napalmed here on November 21, 1950, is now ten years old. Kim Choi Yun looks like a hideous, worn-out old man.

Quite bald, with a white scalp pitted and blotched with red and blue marks, his face is knotted and crinkled. Discoloured scar tissue and flesh around his red-rimmed eyes has been so distorted that he has not shut his eyes since he was burned.

His handsome widowed mother told me he can sleep fitfully in a darkened room, but always with his eyes open.

After he was burned, it was four months before he could get up. He lay for two months between consciousness and death, with yellow pus pouring from his face and scalp.

"Only his youth saved him," the mother said.

"He was such a good-looking boy. Now, look. Who would think he must always be like this, ugly, hairless, sleepless?"

Kaesong was a South Korean town whose citizens the Americans claimed as their supporters.

Mrs Kim Yang Sun, who lives nearby, was napalmed in the last raid here before the peace talks began – May 29, 1951.

She was cooking a meal when a napalm bomb burst near the kitchen door, spraying her with molten fire. She was burned to the bone on the face, back, hands and feet, with deep destruction of flesh on the buttocks.

Today, she was all the time scratching and rubbing her burns, which still feel like fire, and itch unbearably a year later.

On her back an enormous purple scar, one foot wide by nine inches long, is raised almost a quarter of an inch from the surrounding flesh.

She was helped outside for me to photograph. After a few moments in the sunshine she had to go indoors again. She can sleep for about half an hour at a time before pain awakens her.

After being burned she could not get up for five months. "I only wanted to die," she said.

Both this woman's sons are in the Korean People's Army. She is 58.

These are two of the hundreds of napalm survivors in this town. People condemned to spend the rest of their lives in misery and pain, pitiful, crippled caricatures of human beings.

At any water hole where children play, you can find boys and girls with great scars and still unhealed wounds from the raids last year, children with muscles ruined and thick, stiffened welts on the backs of hands and tops of feet, partly crippled.

It is common to find burned backs of hands and sides of faces – where children have protected their heads instinctively with their hands.

Napalm sticks and burns the flesh below, bringing a horrible death. Attempts to wipe it off simply transfer it to a new place, with no effect on the old.

Its primary use by the Americans has been against the civilian population, for troops are normally protected by skilfully dug positions.

I shall never forget the mother of little Kim Choi Yun, weeping as she held him to her, a tiny child made into a dreadful wizened old man. "Who will ever marry him?" she asked.

'How we dropped the germ bombs'

Alan Winnington, somewhere in North Korea

At 3.30 on the morning of January 4, 1952, a bomber piloted by 1st-Lt John Quinn, of the US Air Force, arrived at a point just south of Pyongyang, North Korea.

Quinn brought his plane down to 200 feet. His navigator, Lt Rogers, told him they were over the appointed spot. He dropped his four wing-bombs.

Quinn said to me later:

"They dropped one at a time in rapid succession. They were 'duds.' We both knew for sure then that they were germ-bombs."

Those were two of the first germ-bombs dropped by the Americans in Korea.

I have been talking to Lt Quinn. His serial number is 17993A and his address 751 East Sacramento Street, Altadena, California.

I have also interviewed Navigator Lt Kenneth Enoch, No AO2069988, of 18 South Osborne Street, Youngstown, Ohio, who also flew in a germ bomber.

Both men were shot down on January 13. Both say they acted on the rule that "orders are orders." Both are ashamed of what they did, and have now tried to atone in some degree by giving statements in their own writing about the germ attacks in which they took part.

Here is part of what Quinn – 29 years old, reddish hair, moustache – told me when I went to his comfortable quarters in a prisoner-of-war camp.

He arrived in South Korea from the United States on November 30, 1951, and was assigned to the 8th Squadron 3rd Group of 3rd Bomb Wing, US Fifth Air Force. His squadron flew B26s and was based at Kunsan, South Korea.

"On December 18," said Quinn, "I went to a lecture with Larson, a navigator. There were 20 in the room, all pilots and navigators. I remember, in addition to Larson, 2nd-Lt Schwartz, 1st-Lt Rogers, 1st-Lt Watson, Capt Long, Capt Duffy – all navigators. Pilots included Capt Howarth, Capt Land, 1st-Lt Schmidt, Capt Robertson, Capt Beeson and 1st-Lt McAllister.

"We were introduced to a Mr Ashfork – a civilian about 40 years old, 5ft 10in in height, slim, going bald.

"Mr Ashfork lectured on biological warfare, which he said was a terrible thing, but we must be prepared to carry it out if necessary.

"Then he described methods of spreading germs through insects and rodents in containers and old clothes, by bombs and by dust.

"He showed us pictures of germ-bombs that looked very much like the 500lb general-purpose bombs that we had been carrying, except that they had no fuses.

"One picture was of a bomb that split in half when it struck the ground. He described others that came apart in the air, scattering boxes over a large area. The boxes became weak in sunlight and insects were able to crawl out."

It was stressed that the bombs carried no explosive charge. Technically, they were "duds."

On New Year's Eve, Quinn attended a routine briefing.

"The only thing not routine," he told me, "was that the briefing officer stressed we must be very careful in future to report any 'duds' to Intelligence section when we reported back."

On January 3, Quinn went, with Lt Rogers as his navigator and a Sgt Sayer as engineer, to another briefing, which also seemed routine. But a few hours later he had a shock:

"Rogers, Sayers and myself met in Group Operations at five minutes before 1am and went into a little room where the alert officer stayed at night. This was a regular procedure in case of last-minute change of orders.

"Capt Reynolds was on duty. He told me I had a special mission. Before I did anything else I was to drop my wing-bombs as close to Pyongyang as I dared.

"He said I should drop the bombs from 200 feet, or lower if possible, and not worry about any explosion as they would be 'duds.'

"I asked him what it was all about – 1,200 feet is usually regarded as the minimum safe altitude for dropping 500-pounders.

"I remembered the lecture we had been given on germ-bombs and the reference to 'duds.'

"Reynolds said he did not know what it was all about, and it would be best just to do as I was instructed and not worry about why or what.

"Then I was certain they were asking me to drop germ-bombs."

When the crew went to their plane they found it guarded.

"This confirmed my suspicion that we were to carry germ-bombs," said Quinn.

"The guard told us not to worry about the wing-bombs as they had already been taken care of. But I looked up at them when inspecting the plane.

"Rogers had told me: 'The wing-bombs don't have any fuses.' He was correct. "We looked at each other, and I said: 'Orders are orders,' and we left it at that.

"We took off at 2.29 in the early morning and arrived just south of Pyongyang at 3.30. I turned east of the road just south of the bridge, and when we reached 200 feet Rogers said we must be at the right spot and I dropped the four wing-bombs."

Quinn's second germ-bomb mission was in the early morning of January 11.

"Capt Reynolds was again on duty," Quinn said. "He recalled that I had already had one special mission, and this would be the same, but there would only be two 'duds.'

"At the plane we were again met by a guard who told us the wing-bombs had been 'taken care of.' I noticed the two outboard bombs had no fuses."

Quinn dropped the two germ-bombs north of Kunuri and again reported them to Intelligence as 'duds.'

He said though they had the strictest orders never to discuss germ warfare, even with their closest friends, he did discuss it with his four room mates and discovered that three of them had been given "special missions."

"When we first found we nearly all had germ missions, we talked about germ warfare and how horrible it seemed," said Quinn.

"We wondered if atomic warfare would be used next, and hoped it wouldn't.

"At that time I agreed with the others that the people who were responsible for giving orders for starting germ warfare must have good reason for doing it.

"I realise how terrible it was to accept such orders as normal, but when you are in the military you get used to just carrying out orders from day to day, no matter what."

Lt Enoch (27 years old, blond, with light blue eyes) attended his first lecture on germ warfare at Iwakune, Japan, on August 25.

On New Year's Day, Enoch was told by Capt Carey, Group Operations Officer, that all "duds" must be carefully recorded.

Enoch took part in a flight early on the morning of January 7 as navigator, with Capt Amos as pilot and Sgt Tracy as gunner.

"Capt Amos and I reported as usual to Group operations office about an hour before take-off. We were told by the officer on duty, a captain not known to me, that we were to fly to Hwangju and drop our two outboard bombs, then dump the rest of the load and return as quickly as possible to Kusan.

"He told us to drop the bombs at 500 feet altitude and a maximum speed of 200 mph. We called his attention to the low altitude as we were carrying ten 500lb bombs, according to briefing.

"But," said Enoch, "he told us that this was a top secret and that these were germ-bombs, and to tell no one whatsoever about our mission.

"He said the wing-bombs were already loaded and checked, and not to bother about them, but to report them as 'duds' when we returned.

"When we got out to the plane there was a guard.

"We took off at 3am and flew to Hwangju, getting down to 500 feet, and dropping two germ-bombs outside the west edge of the town. There were no explosions."

On January 10, with the same crew and in the B26 bomber – No 247 – Enoch went on another bombing mission, and this time dropped four germ-bombs in the outskirts of the town of Chunghwa.

Daily Worker, Tuesday 6 December 1955

My first sight of legendary Lhasa

Alan Winnington, Lhasa, Tibet

Imagine driving in an open car to Nottingham about the time of Robin Hood and you can get some impression of the last miles to Lhasa along the new road from China.

In sparse barley fields, peasants with long matted hair, dressed in unbleached homespun, patched and shapeless, lean on their hoes to watch the car. Women with open bodices feed their babies or scream anxiously as some urchins dare each other to cross in front of the jeep.

When we wave, the peasants touch their forelocks and put out their tongues in greeting.

We come to a section where Tibetans are working on the road for wages, a rare thing in Tibet. As we fly past they jump and clap their hands. They lack the subservience of the peasants.

Slipping through valley after valley, the new road follows the river past monasteries and stone-built houses of the rich.

A splash of bright colour in the distance turns out to be a noble-woman with an escort of three gallants, who pass us waving, with their harness jingling.

Alan Winnington's journey through Tibet in 1955 was undertaken at a time when Tibet had just rejoined China after decades of imperialist interference, which had been ushered in by the notorious British expedition of 1904. Winnington describes the transformation of a decaying feudal system, under which the wheel had not been introduced as a means of transport, and the possibilities opened up.

This article was one of a series which appeared in the Daily Worker in December 1955, as the precursor to a book, Tibet: Record of a Journey, *which Winnington dedicated to "His Holiness the Dalai Lama, His Serenity the Panchen Lama, and all the people of Tibet,*

What seem to be motor cars on legs are men carrying the big light boats of yak-skin stretched on a frame. Enormous ravens hop lazily out of the way but mastiffs remain sleeping, exactly in the middle of the road.

In the distance is a black rain-cloud, with the sun behind it sending out blinding rays that hide everything below in darkness. Suddenly the sun comes through, lighting up the whole valley.

And there in front is Lhasa – legendary Lhasa – with the golden-roofed Potala Palace dominating the whole landscape and making the mountains themselves seem insignificant.

I had come 1,500 miles by jeep to reach this city and it was a moment I shall never forget. I can understand the feelings of a pilgrim after walking the same distance when he first sees the Potala, where the Dalai Lama lives, and knows that he has at last reached his goal.

Lhasa, 1,200 feet above sea level, is the capital of the Tibetan region of China, seat of the local government headed by the Dalai Lama and holy of holies for Lamaists everywhere.

Splendid as the city is from afar, at close quarters there has clearly been little change in sanitation and layout since the 7th century.

That was when Tibet's most popular king married a Chinese princess and set up house where the Potala now stands.

It is a city of religion, aristocracy and commerce and their counter-parts – pilgrims, serfs and beggars.

Until the new power station is completed, a tottering old 100kw generator, which was repaired by the People's Liberation Army, supplies a limited number of flickering bulbs part of the day.

---

clerics and laymen, aristocrats and commoners." Indeed, a picture of Winnington alongside the Dalai Lama and Panchen Lama was to appear on the front page of the Daily Worker.

Winnington describes the book as "a brief account of a journey of some 4,000 miles across the Tibetan plateau," during which "I probably saw more of Tibet than any foreigner saw before, mainly owing to the convenience of using the new roads and to the fact that I was a guest of the two Grand Lamas of Tibet and the Chinese Government."

Winnington's memoirs, Breakfast With Mao, *are highly critical of subsequent Chinese policy in Tibet and of Maoism in general.*

Lorries are now bringing tea from inland China and the price of this Tibetan essential has now gone down.

Shanghai cigarettes, vacuum bottles and other consumer goods are popular, but yaks and camels still toil into Lhasa daily from India and Nepal with lightweight luxury goods sewn up in the skins of their departed brothers.

In this town, that never saw a wheeled vehicle before last year, the most obvious thing is traffic. It simply was not designed for anything but men on foot and horseback. Its narrow, winding streets become quagmires at the least hint of rain.

I turned my jeep into one street the other day to find myself facing a convoy of tea lorries from inland China. I stopped, the crowd closed in to examine the foreigners and that was that.

It took an hour to sort out the traffic jam. But even to write of a traffic jam in Lhasa seems unthinkable.

Apart from traffic there are many signs of the new road's effect. Some of the new things might have got here without the road. Maybe a bank could ride on horseback, perhaps even a post office.

Without the road it would not have been possible to equip the hospital, experimental farm, schools or newspaper.

In the case of the Tibetan language newspaper, there was not even any Tibetan type until the first was cast in Peking.

Among the wealthy here, it is fashionable to use steel girders in the ceilings of houses. Formerly these were shipped in sections of less than a yard long and then bolted together, because a yak can carry only 120lb.

Now the new bridges over the river at Lhasa and Shigatse, as well as many others on the road, are of steel girder construction.

As yet the new things are hardly visible on the surface. The main streets of the town are still as they were: covered with stalls, with dogs sleeping in the remaining patches of sunlight: pilgrims, dervishes and beggars twirl prayer wheels and beg – very successfully, I understand.

From my window I can see women and children carrying water up to the top of the 900-foot high Potala, for every drop of water here has to be carried still.

Down below high officials in their gold robes and hats go clanking past on Mongolian ponies, escorted by half a dozen servants in red-fringed hats like electric lampshades.

On the other hand, I see on the plain below a team of Tibetan footballers practising. For a mixture of the old and the new, I advise watching a football match here.

I saw one the other day – Lhasa versus the People's Liberation Army. It was an accidental draw, for the Tibetan team was a shade better.

It consisted of monks with shaved heads and laymen with their long plaits, as usual done up in two buns on top and a gold ornament between them. The match was refereed by a lama monk in his robes.

The Lhasa captain told me afterwards, in English he had learned in Darjeeling:

"Football was prohibited here before the liberation. When His Holiness (the Dalai Lama) took over temporal power he sent a delegation to Peking to negotiate the agreement by which we rejoin the motherland. He also lifted the ban on football. It is now our favourite sport."

But the altitude puts me out of it. I ran 20 yards with a ball the other day and lost my breath for five minutes.

Daily Worker, Wednesday 15 February 1950

Man on the run

Ruth First, Johannesburg

In the yard of the house we visited the man we were looking for was not to be found.

The people helped us search for him, then someone volunteered an explanation.

"There has just been a police raid here. He is probably hiding," and she pointed into the veld adjoining the rows of houses.

It was usual, they said, for him to run and hide there when the police came.

We remembered that on the way we passed two carloads of police.

A criminal? Well, a man without his passes in order.

We left on our way back to town.

Driving towards the hospital we thought of looking for him in the queue waiting before the outpatients' department. There was a chance he would still be standing there from early morning, when he had gone to have his medicine repeated.

He had missed the raid. A few minutes later he emerged from the hospital gates.

We sat down on some boulders on the pavement to hear his story.

In his shirt pocket was the empty medicine bottle, waiting to be refilled.

In his hands a pouch from which he drew two tattered documents, folded and refolded again till they were crumbling, kept carefully in a pocket for months and years on end, as Africans have to keep documents.

A note from a farmer in the Springs district saying he had completed his service.

Several articles by the South African Communist Ruth First appeared in the Daily Worker at this period, when the apartheid system was being entrenched.

A pass with a police stamp permitting him to report to the office of a court prosecutor in Johannesburg.

Before him, on the grass, his hospital card, recording: "Headache, pain in chest, cough... nose deformation, the result of a mine accident."

From Basutoland he had come to the Rand mines in 1934. He worked at Randfontein, Springs, Rand Leases, City Deep. "A long time," he said.

In 1944 he left the mines, found work in the city, eventually with a firm of house painters.

Then he fell ill. He couldn't be sure when the continual pain in the chest and the cough had started.

He had coughed blood. Miners' phthisis? Possibly.

During this illness he lost his job and lay at home waiting to recover.

One day he got up from his bed, walked slowly to the hospital for medicine.

On the way back, as he was returning along the road in which we were standing, a few blocks from his room, he was stopped by the flying squad.

The passes for his previous job were of no use now.

This man was one of those taken to the Native Commissioner's Court and offered the alternative of serving a jail term, for a pass offence, or working for a farmer.

He found himself among a group of men taken out to a farmer's lorry parked outside the court.

For the next six months he worked on a farm in the Springs district, planting and digging up potatoes, reaping mealies, weeding.

To save his clothes he wore a sack during those months.

He signed no contract. The work began at five in the morning and ended at five or six in the evening.

The workers slept in a small compound. They were locked in at night.

"Plenty ran away," he said.

"You didn't?"

"I was sick. I could not take a chance."

The six months on the farm were "hell," he said simply.

"We had no rest in the day. They make you run even when you work. Foremen all the time.

"There was no chance to eat properly in the middle of the day. They kick you. Force you up when you collapse."

He had fallen in the fields several times, he said, and was forced up each time.

"There was no time to wash. The food was eaten from the ground. No bowls or plates."

"Cold at night?"

"Oh-ho," he said. "No blankets, only sacks." They came in cold from the fields and crawled straight under the sacks.

The six months over, he received £3. Also the note from the farmer and one from the police to Johannesburg.

He wants to work but he has no passes, nor can he get any.

Even should he find a job he would probably not be registered under the new regulations which give the city council, out to control the "influx," power to refuse to register a man even though he may have employment in the city.

A trip to town to find work, to plead for a pass to seek work, will most likely result in a trip to jail.

On the way or at the pass office he might meet the police. The council wants no more work-seekers.

"Surplus Natives" must work on the farms is the order.

Knowing the working of the pass laws he stops in the location, runs when the police appear at the street corner.

He is a man beccme a rabbit, ever furtive and hiding.

Daily Worker, Wednesday 31 March 1954

A great disaster for the French army

From Wilfred Burchett, Somewhere in Viet Nam, Tuesday

The action now taking place at Dien Bien Phu is the most tragic failure for French arms in the whole disastrous fiasco of the Navarre plan to crush the people of Viet Nam.

To the heavy losses in manpower must be added the destruction of French air power which makes this battle one of the costliest of the whole "dirty war" to the French.

The broadcast message of General Navarre, who is French Commander-in-Chief in Indo-China, to General Vo Nguyen Giap, the commander of the Viet Nam People's Army, asking permission to land planes at Dien Bien Phu to remove French wounded, underlines the cost of this battle to the French Expeditionary Corps.

Every French soldier killed or wounded in this battle is the direct victim of the Navarre Plan. The fact that the battle is taking place at all is a reflection of the utter bankruptcy of the plan and the French military position in Indo-China.

The belated attempt of French and American propagandists to present the battle as a "decisive action" launched by the Vietnamese People's Army as an all-out trial of strength with the French Expeditionary Corps is a crude distortion of truth.

The annihilation of several battalions of the cream of the

The radical Australian journalist Wilfred Burchett often contributed to the Daily Worker in the early 1950s, most frequently from Korea, where he reported in tandem with Alan Winnington. During the '60s, the paper carried features by him from Vietnam.

This report, some fortnight into the 55-day battle of Dien Bien Phu, conveys the full scope of the military and political disaster befalling the French imperialists.

expeditionary corps and the destruction of over 100 planes since the beginning of March is the result of Navarre putting his head deep down inside the lion's mouth.

Dien Bien Phu in November of last year was just another quiet, orderly village deep in the liberated area of North-West Viet Nam.

It was inhabited by a small number of people who cultivated rice-fields and tended their cattle, pigs and poultry.

On November 20 last year the French dropped several battalions of parachutists.

Their first action was to round up all the inhabitants of Dien Bien Phu and the surrounding villages and concentrate them in two centres – Dien Bien Phu and the village of Hang Cang, four miles to the south.

At the point of bayonets and menaced with machine-guns, the villagers were forced to construct two airfields and build a fortification, haul wood from the forests and carry out other work.

Why did Navarre choose Dien Bien Phu as the centre to drop his parachutists and construct a fortress?

Navarre had several reasons. To the north lay Laichau, the only important French stronghold in the whole of North Viet Nam, apart from the Hanoi-Haipong region in the Red River Delta.

To the north-west is Phongsaly, important French bastion in the state of Laos and astride the river communications to Luang Prabang, the capital of Laos.

Navarre feared attacks by the Viet Nam People's Army against Laichau to the north and by Lao liberation forces against Phongsaly to the south.

Navarre planned to use troops at Dien Bien Phu to reinforce units in either direction, and if the worst happened, to withdraw from Laichau to concentrate all forces at Dien Bien Phu for counter-offensive actions against the Thai country in North Viet Nam.

The latter was one of the integral parts of the much-boosted Navarre plan.

Navarre concentrated 13 battalions in three groups, but almost immediately the Viet Nam Liberation Army surrounded the area and completely cut the whole force off from the outside world – except the air.

They then captured Laichau, completely wiping out four battalions and over 30 companies stationed in Laichau and at fortified posts elsewhere in Laichau Province.

The whole province, including its capital, was liberated by mid-December, and attempts by the French Expeditionary Force to break through to rescue were halted by the encirclement of Dien Bien Phu.

Phongsaly was captured on February 24, when the whole province was liberated.

The occupation of Dien Bien Phu had failed miserably. The two bastions it was supposed to protect were captured.

The only result for Navarre was to bottle up 13 battalions of his best troops in complete negation of his plan to accumulate "mobile reserves" and conduct large operations in areas already liberated by the Viet Nam People's Army.

The original plans had to be abandoned. The dilemma facing Navarre was how to extricate his troops and avert the greatest disaster French arms had yet suffered in the "dirty war" in Indo-China.

By the end of February there was no longer the slightest military justification to maintain the fortress. At that time he could still have evacuated by air.

But with the Geneva Conference looming up, the decision was made to sacrifice battalions for prestige purposes.

Dien Bien Phu and its outposts are situated in a narrow valley about 15 miles long and surrounded by fairly high hills. The Viet Nam People's Army was formerly entrenched in the hills overlooking the fortress and two aerodromes.

By the beginning of March the besieging forces had already dug an extensive system of trenches and fortifications which pushed nearer and nearer to the French positions.

Navarre began boasting that his forces were about to break out of Dien Bien Phu and launch an offensive into the surrounding countryside.

But the Vietnamese entrenchments and fortifications in the hills and forests prevented any such actions.

The French forces, comprising the Foreign Legion and North African and puppet Thai battalions, launched attack after attack to the north, west and east with no success.

It became more and more clear that, far from any hope of starting an offensive, Navarre's troops were making desperate attempts to flee in any direction and through any point where they could pierce the iron chain of defences.

On March 4 and 5 there were attempts to break out to the east, but each time they were repulsed with over 100 casualties.

The French were equipped with about a dozen tanks and 155 and 105 millimetre artillery and plenty of mortars. Bomber and fighter planes ceaselessly tried to pound Vietnamese positions with bombs and napalm.

American B26 bombers and American Bearcat and Hillcat fighters dropped hundreds of tons of bombs and thousands of gallons of flaming petrol, but the Vietnamese trenches crept slowly but surely down from the forest and hillside toward the French outposts.

American Dakotas were landing every few minutes on Dien Bien Phu and Hang Cang airstrips, bringing in everything from shells to drinking water for the troops whom American policy had demanded must be sacrificed in its prestige stand.

Daily Worker, Monday 26 November 1956

A suit and five hand-grenades

Charlie Coutts, Eye-witness in Budapest

Were there really organised fascist groups in Hungary? It is a question around which many people are arguing the issue of whether the Kadar Government should or should not have asked for Soviet help.

Not only were they there, but it was only by a miracle I escaped the fate of so many of the Hungarians wiped out in the terror.

When the fighting began again after the Soviet troops came in on Sunday, November 4, I was caught on the Buda side of the Danube, which divides the city into two. My hotel was on the Pest side, but it was just impossible to cross the river as there was fighting around every bridge. I stayed the night in a cellar with some Hungarian friends, while a battle raged outside.

On the Monday morning there was a lull and I decided to have another go. The Stalin bridge and Margit bridge were both impassable, so I decided to try for the Kossuth bridge via Moscva Ter, one of the main bus and tram centres.

At first the Ter seemed deserted. Suddenly a hail of bullets came

---

The Soviet intervention in Hungary in the autumn of 1956 caused bitter divisions at the Daily Worker. Peter Fryer, the paper's reporter on the spot, who sided with the insurgents, resigned over the issue, as did the paper's cartoonist Gabriel, and other reporters and feature writers including Malcolm MacEwen, Phil Bolsover, Llew Gardner, Leon Griffiths and the television critic Alison Macleod, who decades later published a detailed memoir of the episode, The Death of Uncle Joe, *which is hostile to the paper's line of support for the Soviet intervention and the government of Janos Kadar. Peter Fryer's contemporary account of his experiences was published as* Hungarian Tragedy.

Charlie Coutts, a British Communist journalist who was present in

from the roof tops and top storeys of the high building on the north side of the square.

Soviet tanks on the south side opened up cannon fire in reply, and from my left two anti-tank guns started up from positions the Hungarian insurgents had dug in the grass of the flower beds that used to brighten the tram terminus.

That was the red light for me, and I dived for shelter in the next street. Seeing a doorway, I ran inside and found myself in a group of about 20 armed men. At once I knew these were a different proposition to the majority of people one saw with arms.

Usually the ages were fairly young, sometimes even 14- and 15-year-olds. This group were all over the 35 mark, well armed with light machine guns.

Two of them approached and asked what I was doing. In my limited Hungarian I told them I was Ujsag Angol – English journalist.

Thinking to take the offensive I told them I was trying to get back to the Palace Hotel to join my friends there – and was there a telephone in the building?

They ignored that and demanded – documents? I showed my passport. No one was very impressed. The two who came up to me had made up their minds I was a Russian. Vehement protests from me of my pure British stock were cut off as one of them pushed the barrel of his machine-gun into my stomach until the sweat ran down the back of my neck.

They began to argue among themselves until one older man took the passport and examined it. He apparently could read a word or two of English and convinced the others that it was in fact British.

Now another intervened and said: "Even if he is he must be a

Budapest during the events, presented a very different assessment in a series of articles which appeared in the Daily Worker in November and December 1956. They were highly critical of the Hungarian Communists and, in particular, the AVH secret police, but reached a very different analysis of how the contending political trends developed with events.

Coutts, who died in 2000, contributed an article to the Morning Star the previous year on Hungary's plans to join NATO.

Communist or he wouldn't be here." I must admit I didn't at the time know the expression for shoot him, but that's what they were saying all right.

Then they began to ask if I had another document (masik document). I played dumb now because even a visa issued by the Nagy Government could have been fatal with this crew.

Thinking to relieve the tension a bit I put down my hand and pushed aside the gun barrel, summoned up a bit of a smile and indicated that it was hardly necessary. It was a mistake. He rammed it back with all his force and doubled me up.

Now his friend began to go through my pockets and my real fear began of what would happen when they came to the visa and identity card in the inside pocket of my jacket.

While this had been going on the older man, who had first accepted I was British, had been arguing with the others. I caught the gist of what he was saying. The argument was that it would be better not to risk anything with a foreigner especially one from Britain from whom they were hoping help might come.

His argument carried weight and the one who was searching my pockets stopped and waved me to the door. I walked as slowly as I could to the street and round the corner then ran just as hard as I could to get back to the comparative safety of the cellars.

This was one of the many well organised groups that had been appearing more and more openly in the streets in the days immediately before Kadar formed his government. Of course it would be a mistake to think that they had only appeared in the last few days before the Soviet troops came in for the second time.

Take the case of the sinister figure of Joseph Dudas, who has been mentioned in the Western Press as leader of one group of fighters. It is interesting to know a bit about the man.

His name first appeared in Hungarian history when Admiral Horthy wanted to conclude in 1944 a separate cease-fire with the Soviet Union.

He contacted the illegal Communist Party and asked them to send two representatives in a five-man delegation to Moscow. The party replied that it would agree if Horthy would give them 5,000 weapons for class-conscious workers to fight the Nazis.

Naturally, that was the end of the contract for Horthy, but he still sent a five-man delegation to Moscow, two of whom claimed to be members of the Communist Party. One of them was Josef Dudas, an engineer.

At the end of the war, Dudas appeared again, working in a factory in Budapest and now actually joined the Communist Party. When the 1947 elections were held, however, he turned up as a candidate for the Smallholders' Party.

Next time he was heard of was during the first week's fighting. At the head of an armed group he went to the National Bank, burst in, and carted off one million forints.

In Izabella Ter he distributed it to all who came and, of course, invited them to join his "Freedom Fighters." Later he went to one of the big clothing outfitters in Rakoczi Ut and took the stocks. This time he issued to all who wanted them a suit and five hand-grenades each.

I saw this issuing of clothes but must confess did not at the time realise its significance. Even the Nagy government of that period did, however, realise what it meant and Dudas was arrested.

He was only in prison for a matter of hours, for by this time the Minister of Armed forces was Kiraly who, incidentally, had been an officer in the old Horthy army and managed to stay an officer after the liberation. Kiraly ordered the release of Dudas.

When Nagy heard this he described it as treason. But Kiraly didn't wait to defend his actions. He left Budapest and joined a group of fighters outside the city.

That was one side of the picture. The other side was one of the organised groups of youth and students, sincere and out for very different aims. I made my first real contact with some of their leaders on Monday, October 29.

We had met two of the young armed students in the street and one of them was a young lad who had translated for me in a youth meeting and with whom I had become friendly over the past year. He was dressed in a leather raincoat, wearing a beret, the national colours on an armlet, with a tommy-gun slung over his shoulder. We asked him if he could take us to interview some of the leaders of the revolt.

They took us to the Faculty of Law. A portrait of Lenin was hanging just inside the door. Inside, where only ten days before moot legal points were debated dispassionately, the talk was now of how to handle machine guns and restore order in the streets.

This was the headquarters of the Budapest Students' Revolutionary Committee. Leader of the committee was the Communist Ferencs Merey, Professor of Psychology. Other members included assistant professors and students.

Merey explained that the committee was actually formed on the evening of Tuesday, October 23, when some of them met after the demonstration outside Parliament to consider their next steps. While they were talking they got word from the radio that fighting had broken out between Security Police and demonstrators.

On the spot they decided to continue as a permanent committee. On the following Thursday they formed themselves into the Students' Revolutionary Committee in arms.

What were the aims for which they had been fighting? "For a really independent, democratic Hungary building Socialism."

Did that mean they thought there had to be a new party in Hungary, for example, a new Communist and Workers' Party?

"Not at all. We stand by our original demands for the immediate convening of a congress of the Hungarian Workers' Party. Elections at every level. Open and democratic discussion of past mistakes and practices. The hammering out of a new constructive national programme."

What about the troops still fighting?

"We are not responsible for them, but we can't do anything about it. Neither we, the army, nor the police will do more than keep order until such time as Soviet troops are withdrawn from Budapest."

Were these the views of the whole committee and all who support them?

"Absolutely, we are not out to change the basis of Hungarian society, but we need the kind of Socialism and Communism that really corresponds to what Hungarians want. We are all united on this."

What have you been doing these past few days to help restore order?

"Last Thursday the joint committee (formed from the students and intellectuals) sent a delegation to meet Imre Nagy. We presented our demands, much the same as the original 14 points, plus two more: immediate withdrawal of Russian troops from Budapest and the abolition of the Security Police. He did not accept all, but enough to make a cease-fire possible. From then on we worked all out for peace.

"Yesterday morning we began negotiations with the police for the setting up of a national guard. Last night the negotiations were finalised and today we are enrolling students and arming them with weapons received from the police."

So there it was. Two sides of the picture and certainly on the face of it reason to hope that reaction was by no means sure of a victory. What happened to swing the balance in their favour and what were the different factors that made their success inevitable? The days that followed held the answer.

Gunmen on the loose

Charlie Coutts, Eye-witness in Budapest

Between the end of October and November 3 there was an apparent development of democracy. The Smallholders, Social Democrats and National Peasant Party were all re-formed.

Each one declared the need for guarding the achievements of People's Democracy.

No matter how sincere this may have been in the minds of many of its supporters, the Smallholders would soon have been taken over by reaction, if it had not indeed already been taken over. It was to this party that Cardinal Mindszenty would almost certainly have given his support.

The Social Democrats would have been against any tampering with the social ownership of the factories but they were hardly a real political force.

As I watched them all commandeer cars, buildings and begin negotiations with Nagy I couldn't help feeling that now the old politicians were coming out to reap the benefit of the struggles of the youth and students.

There were other parties appearing too.

On November 1, I spoke to a Nepszava journalist, who had been full of optimism that the revolutionary committees which were being set up in every district and the councils appearing in all factories and offices would come together to prevent any return to the Horthy regime.

Now he was plunged in despair after attending a meeting in Buda where 600 people had met to set up a district revolutionary committee.

At the start, with a trade unionist in the chair, the feeling had been very good. Everyone felt the aims of the struggle had been won and that with the withdrawal of Soviet troops they could begin to put the aims into practice.

This atmosphere was short lived.

Forty young armed men came in accompanied by a priest.

Their spokesman told the meeting that they intended to form there and then a new political party – the Christian Party.

Naturally, there were no vocal dissenters.

Then they proposed candidates for the revolutionary committee, and, equally naturally, they were all elected.

This is, of course, an extreme example, for in most cases one only had to have a weapon to have been a Freedom Fighter and get elected, or, to be more correct, appointed. However, it does show how reaction was working behind the facade of democracy.

In the factories it could not have been very different. At many places at first the workers had defended their factories against all comers.

Their attitude was: these factories are ours and no one will damage them, neither Hungarians nor Russians. In places like Stalinvaros they went farther and declared their readiness to struggle to remain Socialist cities.

Quite a number of factories reported electing Communists to their councils – but by the last week all the forces of reaction were aiming to win control in the factories with both terror groups and demagogy.

Needless to say, in every field reaction had a tremendous area to work in, for there is no doubt that there was mass anti-Soviet feeling and that the old Hungarian Workers' Party was rejected.

Reaction was coming out on top because among the workers there was no organised party to oppose it.

The new Hungarian Socialist Workers' Party was little more than leaders; the Social Democratic Party was in the same boat. This, then, was the opportunity to smash completely any possibility of the working class finding independent leadership.

I have read in various papers that most Western journalists felt that White Terror had practically ended by November 1. In my opinion it was only getting under way.

On Friday November 2 a Swedish journalist and I were in Bazja Utca.

A young man with the inevitable tommy-gun was standing in the middle of the road looking up at the windows of a block of flats.

Another one joined him carrying a piece of paper.

They both looked at it, obviously decided they had found the right address and went inside. We walked on and as we turned the corner there was a single tommy-gun burst from inside.

Only then did we realise that we had seen one of the many instances of the murder of individuals in their homes by people using lists of names and addresses.

You might ask why decent people didn't stop it.

They didn't first of all because the national sentiment was so deep that every armed man was regarded as a patriot. Secondly they were now really bitter in their attitude to the Hungarian Workers' Party.

Thirdly, because for most people it was difficult to see the extent of the terror.

You might, for example, only see one incident such as we witnessed. All transport was off and so one could really know only what was happening in one's own immediate district.

To add to the confusion there were now at least twenty different newspapers being distributed – all carrying different accounts of the same events.

On every wall there were posters, slogans and demands.

They ranged from properly printed work to hand-written notes of the latest "News" from Radio Free Europe. The thing that marked all these reams of paper was the fact that each day they became more and more hostile to Socialism.

On Saturday, November 3, the day before the Soviet troops returned, a demand of great significance appeared. It came from the "National Committee."

This group had led an attack on the Workers' Party rooms in Lenin Korut. They set up headquarters there with loudspeakers and machine-guns mounted side by side in the windows overlooking the main street. Across the road they parked what appeared to be their "own" Hungarian Army tank.

By loudspeaker, leaflet and newspaper they now advanced the idea that the Nagy Government was incapable of governing (very true, of course) and that until general elections could be held, a new Government should be formed by the army.

Linking that with the role of Colonel Maletar – now Minister of

Defence – and the other colonels whose names were constantly associated with all these events, I found this one of the most convincing proofs that a coup d'etat was just round the corner.

So in the day before Soviet troops came in my thoughts had reached the stage where I could see nothing but fascism as the inevitable outcome of the past tragic 11 days.

These days began in high hopes of changed policies in answer to the demands that Socialism in Hungary should correspond to what the Hungarian people wanted and the mistakes and crimes of the past should be put right.

Now they looked like ending in the loss of every hard-won gain of the working class and establishment in central Europe of the trouble spot from which a new world war could start.

I looked at the Government and saw no hope there. Nagy was ready to change his Ministers once again and everyone was aware that nobody could carry out his edicts any way.

The role of Colonel (now General) Maletar, top man in the armed forces and Civil Guard, was not one to inspire confidence.

The students? Their revolutionary committees seemed sunk in despair at the way things had turned out. Those who only last week had been talking of how they were leading the national movement now had no control over events at all.

The workers' councils in the factories, in many cases neutral, in others led by reaction, in others led by good honest workers, were all without any central leadership.

This was the time when those who knew what they intended to do could brush aside all opposition and walk into power. And the only force capable of stopping them – the Communist Party – was blown to the four winds.

But there were five men who saw that danger and broke with the Nagy Government.

Their leader was Janos Kadar. The responsibility they faced was enormous. They must have known that when they called for the help of Soviet troops it could mean yet another tragedy.

It meant that in the atmosphere of national pride and bitter feeling toward the Soviet Union it would not be reaction alone that Soviet troops, and those units of the army who were with the Government, would have to fight but thousands of young Hungarians who would be honestly thinking that they fought a just cause.

The alternatives were stark, but I believe they chose the right one.

As Hungary painfully takes the road forward again, out of the bitterness and pain of these past weeks, I'm sure more and more workers will see that and realise that fascism was stopped just in time.

Hungary has her second chance to build Socialism – the nation's aim when it took the road of People's Democracy.

Daily Worker, Thursday 13 April 1961

A Communist in space

Dennis Ogden, Moscow, Wednesday

There's a hero's welcome to end all hero's welcomes waiting for 27-year-old pilot-astronaut Major Yuri Gagarin when he gets to Moscow on Friday morning.

News of the "Chelovek v kosmos" – "The man in space" – flashed round the city at cosmic speed this morning. Crowds gathered at loudspeakers in squares and streets to hear reports of his 108-minute flight in the $4^1/_2$-ton space ship called "Vostok" ("East").

Motorists in Gorky Street pulled in to the pavement and turned on their radios to let the people hear the latest news.

A buzz of excitement and murmurs of "molodets" – "good fellow" – greeted the words that the flight was proceeding normally and that Major Gagarin felt fine.

"Good luck to you and may you come back safely," murmured a silver-haired old lady standing by my shoulder.

Students at Moscow University interrupted their lectures and headed to Red Square, already thronged with people. They carried hurriedly written posters saying: "Glory to the Soviet spaceman."

When news winged through the city that the portrait of the first

The Soviet Union marked the achievement of putting a man into space by renewing its appeal for peaceful coexistence. The Daily Worker carried the test on its front page: "We do not place our achievements and discoveries at the service of war, but at the service of peace... Let us end the armaments race. Let us bring about complete disarmament under strict international control." The US response came five days later, with the notorious, CIA-instigated 'Bay of Pigs' invasion of Cuba.

Dennis Ogden had been the paper's Moscow correspondent since 1959. He returned to London in 1962 and later became a lecturer in Soviet politics. He continued to contribute articles to the paper.

spaceman would be shown on television, people in the street knocked at the homes of strangers, eager to see the face of the hero.

Then as the final triumphant news of Yuri Gagarin's safe landing without even a bruise came through, the crowds gathered in Mayakovsky Square, broke into cheers and applause, the almost unbearable tension broken at last.

As the whole Soviet Union went wild with joy, Moscow Radio dubbed Major Gagarin "the Columbus of inter-planetary space."

One woman said over and over again: "I am so glad."

The official Tass announcement ended a period of uncertainty arising from clear indications that such a major space flight was imminent.

"The landing went off normally; I feel fine and have no injuries or bruises," was the message Major Gagarin, on his return from space, asked should be sent to Mr Khrushchov.

"Your flight turns a new page in the history of mankind's conquest of space and fills the hearts of Soviet people with great joy and pride for their Socialist homeland," the Soviet Prime Minister replied by telegram.

"With all my heart I congratulate you on your happy return to earth after your journey in space. I embrace you. Till we meet soon in Moscow – N Khrushchov," the message ends.

Soviet Air Force colleagues are hoping to provide a fighter escort for Major Gagarin when he arrives at Vnukovo airport. There are proposals for a giant celebration in Red Square later on Friday.

A special evening edition of Pravda, normally a morning paper, was on the street today.

News of today's triumph over the forces of nature came in a series of Tass statements, the first broadcast at 10.20am, Moscow time.

"On April 12, 1961, the world's first sputnik spaceship the Vostok, with a man on board, was placed in orbit in the Soviet Union," proclaimed the ringing tones of Moscow Radio's chief announcer Yuri Levitan.

"The pilot of the sputnik spaceship Vostok is a citizen of the Soviet Union, Air Force Major Yuri Alexeyevich Gagarin.

"The launching of the multi-stage space rocket was successful and, after the achievement of the first cosmic velocity and separation from the final stage of the carrier rocket, the sputnik spacecraft began three flights in an orbit round the earth.

"According to preliminary data the sputnik ship's orbital period is 89.1 minutes.

"Its minimum distance from the earth is about 108 miles and the maximum just over 186 miles; the orbit is at an angle of 65 degrees four minutes to the Equator.

"The weight of the sputnik spaceship, including the pilot-astronaut, is 4,725 kilogrammes, not counting the weight of the final stage of the carrier rocket.

"Two-way radio contact has been established and is being maintained with the astronaut," the announcement continued.

"The frequencies of the short-time transmitters on board are 9.019 megacycles and 20.006 megacycles, and in the ultra short wave range 143.625 megacycles.

"The condition of the astronaut during flight is being observed by radio telemetric and television systems. The astronaut, Comrade Gagarin, withstood the placing of the sputnik ship 'Vostok' in orbit satisfactorily and at present feels well.

"The systems ensuring the conditions necessary for life in the cabin of the sputnik ship are functioning normally.

"The flight of the sputnik spaceship 'Vostok' with the pilot, astronaut Comrade Gagarin, aboard in orbit continues," the first announcement concluded.

Then, 45 minutes after launching, at 9.52 Moscow time, Major Gagarin, then over South America, signalled: "Flight proceeding normally, feel fine."

Less than half an hour later, at 10.15 Moscow time, he reported from over Africa: "Flight proceeding normally. I am withstanding the state of weightlessness well."

Ten minutes later, having completed his flight round the earth, according to plan, the braking engine system was switched on and the spaceship began to descend from orbit to land in a pre-determined area in the Soviet Union.

Thirty minutes later, at 10.55 Moscow time, the sputnik spaceship, having successfully fulfilled its research programme, "made a safe landing in the pre-determined area."

Man's flight in space, the final Tass announcement concludes, "opens up impressive prospects for man's conquest of space."

Listeners to Moscow Radio's Home Service heard recordings of the messages the spaceman sent back to earth during his flight.

The voice said: *I see the earth, visibility good. I hear you perfectly. The flight is continuing well. I see the earth. Visibility good… one can see everything. Some space is covered by cumulus cloud.*

I am continuing with the flight. Everything normal. Everything working perfectly. Pressing on. Feeling well. I am in good spirits. I am continuing with the flight. Everything is going well. The machine is working normally.

The newspaper Izvestia reported that the landing was excellent and Yuri Gagarin "walked out to meet the people who spotted him in the sky."

He told them: "The sky is very, very dark, and the earth is bluish. Everything is clearly visible."

Describing his first sight of the spaceman, an Izvestia correspondent wrote: "Stocky, smiling, as only a truly happy man can be. he was coming down the gangway of the aircraft.

"He was wearing light-blue, sky-colour overalls and a flying helmet.

"People struggled to embrace him. Gagarin hugged one of his friends, evidently an old friend who was welcoming him at the aerodrome, so hard that it looked like a small wrestling match."

All today this huge city of seven million has lived under the spell of the first manned space flight.

Strangers smile at each other in the streets and congratulate one another on the great achievement.

In one street group, Colonel Veniamin Nemirovsky said: "We have seen a lot in our time and nothing can surprise us any more. But all will bow their heads to the greatness of this exploit that will rock the world."

A 90-year-old pensioner, Yelena Sarbekova, said: "I have lived a life which will be the envy of many generations. I have lived in the days of horse carriages. I have seen the first aircraft. I have lived to hear about the first atomic ice-breaker and the first manned space flight.

"Today I hail the power, the greatness, the triumph and the justice of the new system which made Russia the most beautiful and advanced country on earth, whose citizen was the first man to soar beyond the bounds of our planet."

World-famed violinist Prof David Oistrakh, who was about to leave for the Moscow Conservatory of Music when the first report was broadcast, said:

"Many of us, artists and musicians, have to deal with mighty and daring fantasy. But what has happened today beats the boldest of dreams.

"I was alive at the beginning of a new era, when man went beyond the confines of his planet for the first time. Today, everyone of us can say that he was lucky to live on this day."

Daily Worker, Saturday 15 April 1961

My morning among the doubters

Alan Brown, Worker's Notebook

How did you find the spaceman era came in? Like almost everybody else you must have felt that man had grown considerably taller over those few short minutes of Yuri's flight.

Almost everybody – but alas, not all.

Within a few short minutes of the announcement, together with photographer Ernie Greenwood, I was out of the office asking the proverbial 'man in the street' what he thought.

Generally, the reaction was warm and generous, but there were the exceptions.

One, a man in his forties, was a sceptic of the first water.

He was "taking it all with a pinch of salt," and was only going to believe it, if he saw a picture of the spaceman getting in, and then out, of his spaceship.

As Ernie commented: "What a touching faith in newspaper photographs."

Eccles (Frank Brown) began to contribute to the Daily Worker in the early 1950s and became the paper's daily cartoonist after the departure of Gabriel in 1956. He continued to draw for the paper for over 30 years until his death in 1986. His twin brother Sid worked for the paper for over 50 years, many of them in the publicity department, until his retirement in the late 1990s. Another brother, Alan, worked as a reporter, succeeding George Sinfield as industrial correspondent in 1967.

'The Americans still want to come here'

Sam Russell, exclusive interview with Che Guevara

Despite American attempts to lull the world into a false sense of security, there is an ever-present threat of American aggression against Cuba.

This was underlined to me by Cuba's Deputy Premier and Minister of Industries, Comandante Che Guevara, in the only interview given by a Cuban leader since the Cuban crisis began over a month ago.

For over two hours, until well past midnight, I discussed the situation with him in his office on Havana's Revolution Square, as he put Cuba's point of view with complete frankness and sincerity.

The olive-green uniform which he, like all other Cuban leaders still wear, the armed guards on the building and the men and women

---

In the wake of the Cuban missile crisis, the Daily Worker published this world exclusive interview.

Sam Russell had worked for the paper since the late 1930s, when he reported from Spain during the last days of the civil war. He was the paper's correspondent in France in the early months of the Second World War, filing an exclusive interview with the fugitive leader of the French Communist Party, Maurice Thorez, in November 1939. Russell became foreign editor of the Daily Worker and Morning Star for many years, until his retirement in 1985.

The Daily Worker had warned of the impending crisis in mid-September 1962, in an article by Russell, 'Kennedy tries brinkmanship.' At the height of the crisis, on 24 October, the paper published an appeal by the Communist Party of Great Britain, 'Hands off Cuba,' which described "Kennedy's bellicose broadcast against Cuba" as "without parallel since Hitler's tirades against Czechoslovakia."

drilling in the streets as I came to his office also underlined the sense of imminent danger which every Cuban feels.

"The rockets have gone," he said, "the Il-28 planes are going. But the Americans still want to come here. They have still not given any guarantee against aggression and make everything dependent on unilateral inspection which we will not accept.

"What is more, the Americans reserve the right to be the sole arbiters as to when they should intervene openly as well as the right to violate our air space whenever they want."

Major Guevara said that therefore the situation was still serious, but what would happen in the future depended on a number of circumstances.

The US was trying to estimate what it would cost to liquidate Cuba and what it would gain from liquidating Cuba and on the results of this estimation would depend the decision on whether they launch their attack.

"In the face of an aggressor like the US there can be no other solution than a fight to the death, inflicting the maximum damage on the enemy."

Major Guevara said that he realised that to some people this might sound highly emotional, but during the days of acute crisis the Cuban people appreciated that they were faced with the threat of atomic annihilation and that their determination to resist meant that they would die because they were in the front line.

"Whether the Americans attack or not depends on their estimate of our internal situation and of the international situation. That is why the solidarity of the peoples of the world is of such importance to us.

"We are under no illusion. We know we cannot exist on our own. We depend on the solidarity of the Socialist camp and of the whole world."

I then asked Major Guevara what was the present state of relations between the Soviet Union and Cuba, especially in view of President Fidel Castro's statement on November 1, that certain misunderstandings or discrepancies had arisen.

"During Comrade Mikoyan's visit," he said, "we went into a great number of questions with the Soviet Union. We discussed frankly and fully and each side put his point of view.

"We know that the Soviet Union is the friend that can help us most and we are convinced that she will continue to help us.

"All we have done is to use our right as an independent party within the framework of the principles of international proletarian solidarity.

"The discrepancies are past and will not be of importance in the future. We consider ourselves part of the Socialist world and absolutely faithful to Marxist-Leninist ideas."

My next question was on the effects of the US economic blockade of Cuba and how she has dealt with the situation.

Major Guevara pointed out that while President Kennedy had announced the end of the so-called quarantine, the economic blockade was continuing and President Kennedy had himself declared that political, economic and other measures against Cuba would be intensified.

He pointed out too that the blockade had been imposed in a number of stages. The first stage was when the US closed its ports to Cuban goods and stopped the export of goods Cuba needed. Then the US asked its allies not to trade with Cuba.

"And now," he continued, "the US is preparing to impose sanctions on those ships, merchants and manufacturers who are trading with Cuba. This will hit Britain most of all.

"There could be further acts in this connection. But we can say that each time we have found ways of overcoming the effects of this blockade policy."

Major Guevara said that it would be ridiculous to pretend that the blockade has not hit Cuba, for her factories and public services are mostly equipped with American and British machinery, which needs spare parts for servicing.

"But if we cannot get these spare parts," he added, "then we shall find other ways of overcoming our difficulties, and we have achieved considerable success in this respect already.

"Of course this will mean hardship for us, but today it is impossible to strangle a country economically. So we shall win through. Of course it will mean that our development plans will have to be modified and be less ambitious."

On President Kennedy's threat to use, apart from political and economic pressure, "other measures" against Cuba, Major Guevara said that this covered the whole field of para-military action.

This includes espionage, sabotage, the dropping of arms and the sending of agents by parachute and small landings on Cuba's long coastline, in fact, "everything short of open war, while reserving the right to resort to open attack

"The violation of our air space continues all the time," he said, "and we have not seen the end of this sort of thing by any means."

Major Guevara then gave me some interesting details about the way in which the Cuban people had strengthened their political organisation in the past year in the face of the growing American threat.

The trade unions, the women's organisation, the Young Communist League, and the mass organisations of the people in the Defence Committees which exist in every street and village have been drawn into the solution of a multitude of questions.

For example, things like rationing, prophylactic health measures (especially vaccination and immunisation of children) as well as ensuring round-the-clock vigilance to protect factories, fields and homes against sabotage and espionage.

The past seven months, however, have been specially significant, for they have seen the beginning of the formation of a new United Party of the Socialist Revolution (PURS) following the removal of the former Communist leader Anibal Escalante for sectarianism and his attempts to create an elite separated from the masses of the people.

At present the political organisation of the Cuban people is the Integrated Revolutionary Organisations (ORI) which was formed out of Premier Fidel Castro's July 26 Movement, the old Popular Socialist Party and the Directorate – which was mainly a students' organisation.

The new party is being formed on the basis of mass meetings being held at all places of work where the workers are invited to choose model workers from among themselves

These are then invited to join the new Party, while the fitness for membership of the new Party of members of the present organisations is also discussed at mass meetings.

This process is continuing at the present time all over the country, although it has been held up somewhat by the mobilisation measures necessitated by the crisis of the past month.

When it is completed by the beginning of next year it is hoped to have created the first nucleus of some 50,000 to 60,000 members and hold the first Congress of the new Party built on the basis of men and women chosen by the people themselves to be the vanguard of Cuba's Socialist revolution.

Regis Debray and revolution in Latin America

Joe Slovo

Moved by what he terms "Fidelista impatience," Regis Debray dismisses Lenin's "theoretical formulae" relating to insurrection as having "nothing to do with the present situation."

It is no longer necessary to wait for conditions for revolution to be fulfilled.

For militants of the "Fidelista generation" the conditions for armed struggle "are given in a general manner." In most of Latin America at any rate, the injection at a vulnerable point of national territory of an armed band of dedicated and heroic men will spread "like an oil-patch propagating itself in concentric ripples through the peasant masses, to the smaller towns and finally to the capital." Priority No 1, therefore, is the creation of insurrectionary "foco."

And what of the political leadership guided by the science of struggle? This, in Debray's scheme of things, is only really vital after the capture of power when the construction of Socialism is on the agenda. It will evolve from the people's army and not the other way about.

Debray is highly critical of existing Communist Parties in Latin America, whose leaders he regards as conservatives and time-servers.

His wholesale rejection of the so-called Left establishment is based

---

Joe Slovo contributed this article to the Morning Star as part of a series examining the new revolutionary ideologies which emerged in the late 1960s. Slovo, the chief of staff of the armed wing of the African National Congress, became general secretary of the South African Communist Party and Housing Minister in the first ANC government.

not so much on his criticism of what he believes to be their past failures, but on the theory that in Latin American conditions, in the phase preceding the seizure of power, the military must be predominant over the political. He thus reverses the traditional approach.

He asserts further that the struggle in a colonial or semi-colonial territory cannot be conducted under the banner of Marxism-Leninism or the leadership of the working class.

With Fanon he believes that the working class is relatively pampered and corrupted by the standards of city life and the peasants – for historical reasons – can only be followers of "propaganda by facts."

The insurrectionary foco is therefore initially staffed by students and revolutionary intellectuals who, because of the social situation of many Latin American countries, have been "assigned the vanguard role."

The foco's military exploits will galvanise resistance from the mass of the population. It becomes the nucleus of a popular movement and the political vanguard "in nuce."

His militaristic logic leads him to an advocacy of the principle that, if possible, military and political leadership should be combined in one person.

The commander-in-chief (and it is no doubt true that collectivism is often harmful to the needs of military action) is also the political commander. A new quality is thus introduced for leadership: that of biological fitness. Very little room here for a middle-aged Lenin!

It is certainly arguable (and Cuba is proof of this) that given certain pre-conditions, armed activity can play an important and even decisive role in hastening the evolvement of insurrectionary conditions. The historical process is obviously connected with what people – expressing themselves in organised activity – do, or abstain from doing.

For example, the South African National Liberation Movement makes no claim that there exists at the moment in that country the sort of nation-wide crisis which would warrant an October-style assault on the central power. Yet, for reasons I believe to be correct, it has undertaken armed activity of the guerilla type.

Lenin, more than most, railed against "mechanically equalised and identical rules of struggle" for differing conditions and nations. His famous "formula" (and he would have been the last to insist on this word) was concerned with the problems of the moment of a general all-round insurrection, and not with the way in which a revolutionary organisation can, by its political and organisational work, help create conditions for the conquest of power.

It is, indeed, conceded by many Latin American Marxists that a failure to appreciate this and a mechanical adherence to the so-called eternal rules of revolutionary struggle has in some situations in the past stood in the way of effective leadership.

But all this is a far cry from the dangerous illusion encouraged by Debray's expansive and over-generalised formulations that the injection of an armed group into a country in which there is severe repression – a group, let me emphasise, with no special ties with the people and one which must initially keep away from them – will of itself, and subject only to its professional skill, lead eventually to the growth of a popular armed movement capable of capturing power, for a number of reasons.

Debray's commitment to focismo is unshaken by the post-Cuban history of the routing and destruction of "half a hundred revolutionary organisations" who, he claims, were prisoners of the Cuban model.

"Revolutionary failure is a springboard," he says. "As a source of theory it is richer than victory, it accumulates experience and knowledge." One of the prime lessons of revolutionary failure is surely that a tactic that leads to it is suspect.

His theory of focismo and his denigration of ideological and political leadership are inter-related concepts. They are based, in the first place, on the historically false and over-generalised idea that the dormant mass will respond in the right way to the heroic actions of a courageous elite.

In the second place he believes that we need not worry over-much about theory and ideology; they will emerge out of revolutionary practice. He invokes the Cuban experience to demonstrate that in the special conditions of Latin America "honest and sincere" revolutionary struggles will lead to the conscious adoption of Marxism.

Whatever special circumstances combined to lead to the creation of a unified Communist party out of the constituents of the victorious army led by Castro and the PSP (old Communist Party), history certainly abounds with proof that it is a rare and almost accidental phenomenon that revolutionary struggles – armed or not – lead to the sort of victory which is desired without the guidance, at all important stages, of a revolutionary political vanguard.

Modern scientific Socialist theory, although it obviously has its roots in the struggle, does not arise directly and spontaneously out of it. The point was made long ago by Lenin that the spontaneous development of the working-class movement leads to its becoming subordinated to bourgeois ideology.

If this is true of workers in direct conflict with the class enemy, how much more application has it to a struggle whose main content is national in character?

Revolutionary struggle, even in colonial or semi-colonial countries, requires the guidance of a theoretically advanced collective leadership.

When specific conditions call for armed activity of a guerilla type, it is all the more necessary to be guided by an experienced political vanguard.

The impressive points made by Debray concerning the tactical difficulties of leading such a struggle from the cities, or the need for the political leadership, or part of it, to join the guerillas in no way support his main conclusion.

Of course, the fact that an organisation calls itself "Communist" does not automatically fit it for this role, nor can it claim exclusive ownership of the revolution except by the calibre of its leadership and actions.

At the same time neither Debray nor any other stranger to a situation has the right to brush aside long-established, indigenous revolutionary organisations, and to carry the burden of continent-wide decisions concerning the commencement of any specific form of action and to guide its development.

To do this effectively needs more than analytical brilliance. It requires an intimate nexus between a leader, a people and a situation.

Even in a continent in which it is generally agreed that armed struggle is the rule and the peaceful way the exception, it is highly questionable to claim that only he is making the revolution who physically confronts the enemy with gun in hand. The leadership of a complex struggle surely involves very much more than this.

A mood of impatience is often an indispensable spur to revolutionary endeavour. It is not always the most effective midwife to revolutionary theory.

The Daily Worker had become the Morning Star on 25 April 1966, after plans to change the name had been announced by the paper's management committee in early January. The intention was to broaden the paper's appeal, while maintaining its political and campaigning stance.

Suggestions for the new name were solicited from readers and a miscellaneous list was printed in the paper on 24 January: "People's Paper, Socialist Daily, Socialist Star, International Man, Advance, Daily Tribune, World Today, Community Response, Daily Round, Calling You, The Daily, Daily Compact, The Citizen, Daily Commoner, Commune, Daily Forum, People's Daily, The Radical, Voice of the People, Daily Messenger, Daily Orbit, Forward, Progress, People's Age, People's World, Daily Clarion, World Tidings, The British Citizen."

One reader, in the modernising spirit, recommended: "In this age of technology, in which our newspaper supports the most advanced social system mankind has devised... a name that will reflect this standpoint – The Rocket."

But one of the earliest suggestions, from a Dunstable reader on 13 January, was the one adopted by special general meetings of the paper's shareholders: "As one of your oldest readers I rather regret the passing of the old name, but suggest, in its place: The Morning Star. A five-pointed star would suggest the continuance of Communist principles."

Master Gunner

Profile of the Week

The new Minister of Labour, Mr Edward Richard George Heath, is not a man to pass over in silence. Nor, like some Tory Ministers recently, to be lightly dismissed.

To leave the Civil Service when plum jobs would soon have been there for his picking and choosing and to walk out of one the oldest firms of merchant bankers to become a Junior Tory Whip were acts which set him off from his fellows.

He is a Tory politician out of the second drawer down. Not quite the right school (Chatham House School, Ramsgate) to be a Topmost Person.

But his Oxford follow-up meant that the upper-class educational sausage machine provided him with sufficient background to get on. In 1937 he was chairman of the Federation of University Conservative Associations and two years later was President of the Oxford Union.

Serving abroad during the war as an artillery officer, he was afterwards to command the 2nd Regiment of the Honourable Artillery Company, Territorial Army.

The 'Profile of the Week' appeared regularly on Saturdays from the inauguration of the 'weekend edition' of the paper in 1954 until the Morning Star succeeded the Daily Worker in 1966.

Edward Heath heeded the paper's advice to pay attention to what it was saying sufficiently well for him to advise young Tories to read the Daily Worker in order to learn what goes on inside industry and strikes, as the paper reported in January 1960.

He also arranged to have the offices of the Morning Star bugged during his time as Prime Minister, as the Cabinet papers for the early 1970s have revealed. But he still underestimated the strength of his opponents.

His aim must have been excellent because in 1951 (the same year in which he became Deputy Government Chief Whip) he was appointed Master Gunner within the Tower of London.

It is said of some men that they learn nothing and forget nothing. But this (d.v.) will never be said of Edward Heath. If it is, then he will be worth nothing to the new Tory Government.

In his most recent post, that of Chief Government Whip, he has for four years been known as the Tory Policeman. One major function of that office is to keep the Tory MPs safely in their pens – perhaps more of a job for a sheep-dog than a policeman.

Another function of the Chief Whip is to be the eyes, ears and nose of the Prime Minister in the House of Commons ("I say, Prime Minister, they've started calling you Pac-a-Mac") so that the Big Chief doesn't get out of touch with the lower strata.

In his new job Edward Heath will find a difference – the difference between a herd of place-seeking, careerist and largely timid Tory MPs, and the millions who make up the British working class and its organisations.

It would pay him quickly to forget the old set of rules and learn the new ones.

We can assure him that he will never have to listen at keyholes to find out what the working class is saying. Let him pay attention to its activities and demands and carefully read the Daily Worker, and he will be fully informed.

He might well take immediate note of the rising mood of the workers for shorter hours and better pay by listening to what the three million engineers and shipbuilders and many more are saying at present.

And he would also do well to forget any dreams of grandeur he may have about putting a law on the trade unions. A policeman is likely to get a different sort of treatment in the workshops than in the Lobby of the House.

Unless, of course, with an increased Tory majority, the Prime Minister has taken him aside and had a few words about attacking the trade unions. In which case we might recall the words of Tennyson in the Ballad of the Revenge: "Sink me the ship, Master Gunner – sink her, split her in twain."

Let us recommend to ex-Master Gunner Heath that he does not underestimate the strength of his opponents in the workshops. And that he always allows for the wind when firing. The prevailing wind today no longer comes from the West.

Morning Star, Thursday 27 July 1972

They're free!

Mick Costello

We've got the dockers out – that was the joyous chant outside the National Industrial Relations Court yesterday.

Demonstrating strikers there had just learnt that the five had been freed.

They were under no illusion that what had forced the climbdown by the anti-union court was the massive strike wave sweeping the country.

Yesterday the Trades Union Congress General Council gave the court and the Government notice that there would be a national stoppage in all industries on Monday if the dockers were not released.

It was only hours afterwards that Sir John Donaldson, NIRC president, announced that the five London dockers were to be immediately released.

He shrouded his decision in legal verbiage which lasted a quarter of an hour, but nothing could disguise the further disrepute into which his court has fallen.

Sharing his discomfiture on the bench beside him were Mr Herman Roberts, ex-industrial journalist, and Mr Roy Boyfield.

Mick Costello's report of the victorious struggle to free the Pentonville Five records one of the high points of the battles against the Heath government and the Industrial Relations Act. The Morning Star had not appeared since the previous Saturday, after the order for the arrest of the five dockers had been made and Fleet Street printworkers joined the mounting wave of industrial action in response.

Costello, who became national industrial organiser of the Communist Party, spent a second spell at the Morning Star as industrial correspondent between 1984 and 1987.

The Eccles cartoon appeared during the three-day week imposed by the Heath government during the 1974 miners' strike.

Sir John was at pains to introduce his retreat with an attack on those who have suggested that neither he nor the Official Solicitor were independent of political and industrial pressures.

About the Official Solicitor, he said: "He enjoys an independent status and carries out his duties as he personally sees fit…

"He is not a political or industrial fairy godmother armed with a magic key which unlocks prisons and solves the problems of Governments, unions or those who defy the law."

He expressed "surprise" that it has been suggested that "by one means or another it is possible to influence" the NIRC's decisions, adding: "No attempt has been made by anyone directly or indirectly otherwise than in open court, to influence our decision."

Meanwhile, in the real world of industry – docks, newspapers, London buses, and in many other industries workers were on strike in protest against the imprisonment of dockers and against the Industrial Relations Act.

The TUC General Council yesterday called for a one-day national strike on Monday. All major unions which were still on the register under the anti-union legislation were taking steps to get off it.

Yesterday the Iron and Steel Trades Confederation announced it was off, following a similar decision by the electricians'-plumbers' union EPTU, immediately following the arrest of the five.

The shopworkers' USDAW, Civil Service Union and the Association of Scientific, Technical and Managerial Staffs' executives are taking steps to deregister following their suspension from TUC affiliation last week.

Yesterday the TUC General Council suspended another three unions from membership – the funeral workers (NUFSO), Scottish Bakers' Union and the Society of Shuttlemakers.

Five Law Lords yesterday decided to re-impose the £55,000 fine on the Transport and General Workers' Union for the action by its Liverpool members in contempt of the anti-union court.

The Liverpool dockers continued "blacking" transport to a container base despite instructions from the National Industrial Relations Court that they should stop this action.

Mr Hugh Scanlon, president of the Amalgamated Union of Engineering Workers, moved the national-stoppage resolution at the

General Council yesterday and was seconded by Mr Jack Jones of the Transport and General Workers' Union.

A counter-move by Mr Roy Grantham of the Association of Professional Executive Clerical and Computer Staff was withdrawn.

This simply called for the repeal of the Industrial Relations Act and sought the release of the five imprisoned dockers to allow the suitable atmosphere in which the Jones-Aldington report on the docks could be properly considered.

The vote for the General Strike was 18 to seven. It is understood that among those who cast their vote against action were Lord Jack Cooper and Mr David Basnett of the General and Municipal Workers Union, Mr Jack Peel (textiles) and Mr Frank Chapple of the electricians/plumbers union.

Letters from the foundry workers' union and the Association of Cinematograph Television and Allied Technicians calling for industrial action were brought to the notice of the General Council members.

In the debate mineworkers' general secretary Mr Lawrence Daly said that a one-day stoppage was not enough, that there was a need for "continuing and widespread industrial action until the dockers are released," but in the interests of unity he voted for Monday's strike.

Other speakers who spoke forcefully for action included Mr Alan Sapper of the ACTT and Mr Terry Parry of the Fire Brigades' Union.

Today the national docks delegate conference meets to discuss the Jones-Aldington report on dockers' employment prospects. It will have to decide whether or not to activate a previous decision to strike for jobs.

After the one-day strike decision, TUC general secretary Vic Feather told journalists that it was "wrong to say that trade unionists do not observe the laws of the land. They do.

"These laws are related to all people." But the Industrial Relations Act was "a politically motivated Act, which strikes against trade unions and trade unionists."

Mr Kevin Halpin, chairman of the Liaison Committee for the Defence of Trade Unions, hailed the release of the five as a result of the "magnificent escalating industrial action."

He went on to warn: "But the battle for the repeal of the Act must go on.

"It was industrial action which achieved the release of the five dockers and industrial action on an even wider scale will be necessary to achieve the repeal of the Act."

He called for stepping up of the campaign for an immediate special meeting of the TUC to activate a massive movement of industrial action to compel the Tories to drop the Act.

Helmets fly outside prison

There were amazing scenes outside the gates of Pentonville prison on Tuesday as thousands of demonstrators demanded the release of the five jailed dockers.

The marchers converged on the gates, which were patrolled by hundreds of policemen, in waves that filled the full width of Caledonian Road.

Suddenly, as the crowds swayed, the police closed ranks in direct confrontation and began to push and hustle the front lines. Within a few minutes half a dozen coppers' helmets were sent hurtling through the air.

While Kevin Halpin, chairman of the National Liaison Committee, was speaking a local bus tried to make its way through the ranks but it was stopped and the driver reversed back along the route he had come.

During these moments there were further scuffles with the police who tried to pull one of the banners apart – an action which prompted Mr Halpin to comment: "The score is now one trade union banner to six policemen's helmets."

A great roar from the crowd greeted the news that French dockers have decided to black all British cargo until the dockers are released.

The demo broke up peacefully with a pledge to mount mass pickets at all industrial establishments not yet involved as part of the campaign to bring shipyards, factories, offices, newspapers etc to a halt.

This was summed up by printworkers' leader Mike Hicks, who told the audience that in stopping Fleet Street they had not "stopped a service to the people but a lie factory."

London docks shop stewards' committee chairman Jim Carpenter told the meeting that the Pentonville Five were in jail "for fighting for the right of free trade unions."

He announced that the National Amalgamated Stevedores and Dockers, which has members among some of the imprisoned men, had made the national dock strike official.

"Only direct action can secure the release of these five dockers," he concluded.

A message was read out from the Pentonville Five, which called on the TUC leaders to "use the strength of the movement to free the dockers," and to "carry out congress decisions in opposing the Act."

London road haulage stewards' chairman Eric Rechnitz warned the Tories: "Keep your pig's snout out of our affairs." – a reference to the use of the Act against dockers, while there was a dispute between drivers and dockers.

Morning Star, Tuesday 25 September 1973

I saw democracy murdered

Sam Russell

I saw democracy murdered in Chile by the rabble of Rip van Winkle generals and admirals recruited by the CIA to impose a savage military dictatorship on a people which had seen and welcomed the dawn of a new era. As I left Santiago at the weekend the rumble of tank tracks, artillery and armoured vehicles through the streets of the capital at first light, heralded the start of a monster man-hunt.

All the anodyne assurances of the first days by this gang of thug generals who have never fought a war except against their own people have now been exposed.

The junta headed by General Pinochet, the treacherous military gangsters who had betrayed their oath of allegiance to the legally elected government headed by President Allende, had hoped that their first display of savagery would cow the people of Chile into silent submission.

But the 36 per cent of the population which voted for the Popular

---

Nearly four years before the Pinochet coup, the Morning Star had published an article by 'A Special Correspondent' in Chile on a failed right-wing coup attempt to forestall a Popular Unity election victory in 1970.

The article, 'Generals and mummies v the people' (11 November 1969), noted: "The right is terrified of the prospect presented by the United Left. It has been watching unhappily every successful step the left has made toward unity... because the right has recognised these developments it has resorted to drastic tactics, and has fomented an atmosphere ripe for a coup d'etat. Nothing would suit the right better than to have the country ruled by a military dictatorship: the capitalist interests would be safe; the present political and economic tie-up

Unity programme of the Socialist, Communist, Left Christian and other progressive parties three years ago and which increased that vote to 44 per cent last March, were not so easily cowed.

From my hotel room across the square from the Presidential Palace of La Moneda I watched on that morning a fortnight ago as the tanks moved into position and began shelling the building at point blank range.

Then came the Hawker-Hunter jets screaming across the sky in a series of rocket attacks which had obviously been well rehearsed and which blasted the building and shook the whole square.

President Allende, warned in the early hours that a coup was imminent and that the Chilean navy was returning to the port of Valparaiso, had left his private residence and arrived at the Moneda to take up his post in defiance of the generals' threats and ultimatums.

From sources close to the murdered president's personal bodyguard, I later learned that, while the attack on the palace was at its fiercest, he declared that he would never betray the cause of the common people of Chile who had elected him, that he would never desert his post and that he would never surrender.

President Allende was gunned down in cold blood by a captain of the army. I have not met anyone in Chile who believed for a moment the suicide story concocted by the army junta.

Not even those Chilean gentry who obscenely opened bottles of champagne to toast the death of President Allende believed the story.

---

with the United States would be maintained; the land would remain in the hands of the powerful latifundia owners, and the danger from the left would be crushed by military force, as is the case, for instance, in Argentina and Brazil. It is also clear that such a government in Chile would also suit the United States... In May 1968, when the first signs of economic discontent in the armed forces came to light, two secretaries of the US embassy in Chile, Wheelock and Yoters, began moving quite openly in Chilean political circles, planting the idea of an eventual coup d'etat as being a way out."

The 1969 coup attempt was defeated by a united mobilisation of the people in a national strike called by the Chilean TUC. But the pattern had been set for a renewed attempt in 1973.

When asked by foreigners like myself about the suicide story, they leered and winked as they swilled the champagne.

In a corner of the basement where guests were later shepherded hotel workers, men and women, boys and girls, wept as the radio blared out the traitor generals' bombast and stared with silent bitterness at the champagne-swilling mob gloating over the murder of Chile's hero president.

On the second day, on one of the deserted upper floors, I came across a small group of other hotel workers gathered round a television set watching the first versions of the junta's doctored story of the coup.

Then came an announcement that any person who had not surrendered to the military by 3pm that day would be shot out of hand.

"Son fascistas," said one hotel worker, and fascists they are.

A reign of terror and mass murder of the finest sons and daughters of the Chilean people, workers, peasants and intellectuals is now under way.

Then the air, artillery and armoured attacks were switched to the working class industrial belt of Santiago, strongholds of the Popular Unity government and its Socialist and Communist Parties.

For weeks the danger of a coup had been there and attempts had been made to ensure defence of the working class areas and of those factories that had been taken over by the workers.

But the brutality and suddenness of the attack caught most workers off their guard, and the heroic resistance was ruthlessly crushed.

Only four days after the coup, I overheard one Carabinero officer of

---

"Sam Russell, Morning Star Foreign Editor went to Chile to report on the growing threat to the Popular Unity government from right-wing and fascist forces.

"He arrived in Santiago the night before the coup, and from his hotel opposite the Presidential Palace watched the murderous attack which ended with the assassination of President Allende.

"Unable to send reports because of the censorship, and refusing to be accredited to the junta of traitor generals who carried out the coup, he has returned to give this exclusive account of events." – Morning Star editorial note.

the armed police say that over 5,000 "Marxists" had by then been killed, of which about 4,000 were in Santiago alone.

Well-known centres of working class militancy like the Sumar and Yarur factories were savagely attacked. Prisoners were shot out of hand in many cases as they came out with their hands behind their necks.

Visiting the areas around these factories a few days later I saw the congealed blood on the pavements. Only 200 yards from my hotel in central Santiago the body of a worker murdered during the night was deliberately left on the pavement all morning while soldiers smoked and joked around the bullet-ridden remains.

Workers in the glassworks of Cristaeerias Chile were similarly gunned down and resistance in government buildings and the Bank of Chile headquarters near the Moneda was crushed.

One of the most horrific accounts of the massacre that was given me by an eyewitness was the slaughter of students at the State Technical University.

When news was received of the attack on the Presidential Palace, a hurried meeting of the hundreds of students and academic staff was called. A decision was taken that armed resistance was not possible.

Nevertheless, armoured detachments which arrived on the campus began opening fire on every window and at anything or anyone that moved.

Students and staff were then rounded up and forced to lay down on the ground face down, with the threat that anyone who moved would be shot.

Then after some hours, officers shouted out that women would be allowed to leave and they were gathered together to be taken off in buses.

As the women stood waiting, the eye-witnesses told me some of the men raised their heads to say goodbye to their wives.

Without warning troops opened up on them with machine-guns… The woman who saw it all said she did not know how many were left there dead and dying as the women were herded into buses and taken away.

The shooting continues, the mass arrests mount every day. I left Santiago before the junta organised its conducted tour of the

National Stadium where thousands of prisoners are herded on the open terraces.

But before I left, the junta itself admitted that about 100 people had been killed, and since then it has been obliged to more than double that figure.

It has also admitted that three prisoners were "shot while attempting to escape" at the Cerro Moreno airport at Antofagasta. Their names were given as Nahad Thedorovic, Luis Alberto Munoz Bravo and Elizabeth del Carmen Balaniz.

In the days before I left, the junta started the mass purge of all government employees.

Vast queues formed outside government offices, banks and headquarters of nationalised industries like the Central Bank of Chile, the Copper Corporation and others.

Troops with machine-guns at the ready stood alongside as the employees inched their way through the doors to be checked by armed police. Heads of offices who had previously been removed because of their failure to carry out their section of the Popular Unity programme were reinstated.

At one such office, I saw police dogs snapping at the heels of men and women as they waited their turn to be "processed" by the junta's trusties.

Soon a stream of people began coming out, women weeping, men grim-faced, while those who hesitated for a moment had the butts of rifles and machine-guns thrust into their backs.

Despite all the junta's suave assurances that there would be no "vengeance," any known supporter of President Allende's Popular Unity government was being sacked on the spot in the ministries.

"Now we have to build a nation of brothers," declared junta chief Gen. Pinochet in a flowery message to the armed forces.

But, at the same time, his fellow traitor, air force chief Gen. Gustavo Leigh, was calling on all people to denounce any known "Popular Unity elements" to the police.

In a declaration two days after the coup, the Cardinal Primate of Chile, Archbishop of Santiago Raul Silva, called for "respect for the fallen, and in the first place for him who was, till Tuesday, September 11, the president of the republic."

Since that declaration, the members of the traitor junta and their stooges in the press, radio and television have not allowed a day to pass without adding to the campaign of lies and denigration against President Allende.

"We call for moderation toward those who were defeated," said the cardinal. "Let there be no reprisals. Let there be taken into account the sincere idealism which inspired many of those who have been defeated."

The traitor generals and admirals who later gathered in church to receive the cardinal's greetings, and who at every turn call on God as their witness and inspirer, have launched a campaign of terror and hate.

But the workers, peasants and intellectuals of Chile who voted so massively for President Allende and the Popular Unity government have yet to have their say.

As the raids on houses all over Santiago continued, the mass arrests, the book burning, the shooting, it was becoming evident that the gang of generals will have more on their hands than they bargain for.

Racism dictates the level of women's oppression

Angela Davis

When the original impetus for the women's rights movement in the United States was created by the campaign to abolish slavery, this was by no means a fortuitous occurrence.

More than a decade before the 1848 Seneca Falls Convention, which placed the issue of women's emancipation on the historical agenda, white working-class women in the cotton mills of New England were comparing their predicament with that of their black sisters and brothers in chains.

Horrendous working conditions, inordinately long hours (sun-up to sun-down) and slave-like wages practically forced these women, who were the country's first factory workers, to conclude that the enslavement of black people had established a pattern of oppression which also claimed them as victims.

As the women in Lowell, Massachusetts were participating in one of the earliest recorded organised strikes, they paraded through the town singing:

> Oh isn't it a pity such a pretty girl as I
> Should be sent into the factory to pine away and die
> Oh, I cannot be a slave
> I will not be a slave
> For I'm so fond of liberty
> That I cannot be a slave.

These working-class women must have recognised that as long as slavery was a reality, the precedent for their own miserable lives would continue to exist.

This article appeared as part of a series of articles on aspects of class, race and women's oppression by the US Communist Angela Davis.

And, indeed, they did not stop at drawing this parallel through their slogans: they made tangible contributions to the anti-slavery struggle.

Among other things, the Lowell women organised annual fairs to raise money for the Abolitionist movement.

Through their solidarity actions the mill women were acknowledging the fact that the enslavement of black people had established general standards of oppression, which were extended, in moderation of course, to white workers, and, in an especially pronounced fashion, to women and children factory workers.

This was the significance of Marx's contention that labour in a white skin would never be free as long as labour in a black skin was branded.

It is impossible to envision the liberation of black people as a people without situating the struggle for economic equality – and eventually the abolition of capitalism – at the core of the liberation movement.

It is equally futile to dream that women as a sex can attain full equality if the economic roots of women's oppression under capitalism are not vigorously attacked.

There is thus a common nucleus around which the two webs of oppression have been spun.

Racism, however, is the more pernicious of the two, as the history of this country so clearly reveals. Since the era of slavery, the level of racism has dictated, in very real ways, the level of women's oppression.

"White women are not free of [racism's] effects: the slaveholder's power over black women's lives and his vicious use of that power established a way of treating all women and a pattern of behaviour toward females which Southern women suffer from to this day.

"The treatment of black or Puerto Rican and other minority women in factories sets the standard for the treatment of all women; if the boss can get by with it (speed-up, lack of safety features, health hazards, etc.) among one group, you can bet he will try to extend it."

Not only has racism determined, in many important ways, the level and intensity of women's oppression, the organised challenge to racism and, in particular, the struggle for black liberation, has dictated the goals and strategies of the movement to achieve equality for women.

It was not an accident that the first man to publicly join the ranks of the women's movement was a black man – the great Abolitionist leader, Frederick Douglass.

Moreover, the Achilles' heel of the woman suffrage movement was its betrayal of the legacy which had been forged by its own origins: the inseparability of the fight for black liberation and the fight for women's emancipation.

After the vote was won for women, it was clear that the capitulation to racism, and, in some instances, the open advocacy of white supremacy, had almost led the suffrage movement to defeat.

Many of the Southern states voted against woman suffrage because they feared it would double the black vote.

This proved that the equally racist argument that had been proposed by suffrage leaders had not, after all, been very convincing.

It had been their contention that once women were given the vote, the enormous number of white women voters would easily cancel the power of the black vote.

"Some day the North will be compelled to look to the South for redemption from (the) evils (of foreigners with their imported customs, greed of monopolistic wealth and the unrest among the working classes).

"Just as the North will be forced to turn to the South for the nation's salvation, just so surely will the South be compelled to look to its Anglo-Saxon women as the medium through which to retain the supremacy of the white race over the African."

These outrageous remarks were made at a major convention of the National American Woman Suffrage Association held in New Orleans in 1903.

When the suffrage movement dismissed the fight for black liberation as either tangential or even detrimental to their cause, this was not the first time the women's movement had been infected with racism.

During the earliest days of the movement, when Sojourner Truth delivered her "Ain't I a Woman" speech, she did so over the objections of many of the women present at the Ohio convention.

These women did not want their movement associated with "abolition and niggers," because they felt it would jeopardise their cause.

It is significant that the more the woman suffrage movement alienated itself from the black liberation movement, the more it failed to represent the needs and interests of white working women.

Just as black women could not isolate the fight for political rights for women from the liberation of black people, so many white working-class women criticised the suffrage leaders for portraying the female vote as a panacea.

"Women workers, who toiled 14 to 16 hours for less than subsistence wages, were more interested in a shorter workday and higher wages than suffrage and property laws."

When the first national black labour organisation came into being, as a reaction to the exclusion of black workers from the existing trade unions, its leaders recognised the need to join the struggles against racism and male supremacy.

In 1869, at a time when the white labour unions were adamant in their refusal to accept women, women were readily admitted to the founding convention of the Coloured National Labour Union.

Moreover, the delegates elected Mrs Mary Carey to their executive committee.

The Committee on Women's Labour recommended: "Profiting by the mistakes heretofore made by our white fellow citizens in omitting women ... that women cordially be included in the invitation to further and organise co-operative societies."

This pronouncement itself was a recognition of the impossibility of effectively defending black workers without a simultaneous defence of the rights of women workers – women workers of all colours.

It was not necessary to be either black or a woman to recognise that in a system dominated by capital's fierce drive for profits, racism and male supremacy, especially when they are taken together, are powerful weapons in the hands of employers.

The brutal economic exploitation of black people justifies and facilitates the over-exploitation of women workers – and the two, in combination, push the capitalists into high gear in so far as their ability to exploit white male workers is concerned.

Sari power

Graham Taylor

On October 1, as workers munched sandwiches outside the factory gates of Willesden, the High Road suddenly exploded into such a blaze of colour as had never before been seen on a Friday lunch time.

Down the road, banners flying, swept hundreds of demonstrators, led by Indian workers. In the vanguard, saris swirling, were the Indian women. Not submissive, house-bound women, but Grunwick strikers, fists raised in anger.

Not the inarticulate, immigrant women we are often told about. Hardly, for at every building they passed they shouted their one, resounding slogan: "Union! Union! We want Union!"

The Grunwick factory, next to Dollis Hill Station, has been described by Laurie Pavitt, MP for Brent South, as "a sweat shop with a management which could have been lifted straight out of the Dickens era."

According to the strikers, compulsory overtime, sacking without notice, wages of £28 for a 40-hour week, no holiday pay, dismissal for those who join a union, raising of the hand to go to the toilet are just a few of the fringe benefits Grunwick offer. The brown labour force, they say, is ordered about by the management with obscene swearing variously intermingled with threats of dismissal.

For two and a half years Mrs Desai worked for Grunwick in these conditions, handling the paperwork for a company that depends almost entirely on mail orders for its film-processing.

This feature on the Grunwick strikers appeared in the Morning Star more than six months before the mass pickets, for which the dispute is remembered, began in June 1977.

Graham Taylor was an executive committee member of Brent Trades Council, continuing the paper's tradition of opening its pages to lay activists, which began with the 'worker correspondents' in the 1930s.

Like most of the workers, Mrs Desai came to England from east Africa and when I visited her on the picket line last week, I found a middle-aged woman slightly built, wearing a yellow sari, with a red spot in the middle of her forehead.

I wanted to know exactly how the strike began, but it was typical of Grunwick dedication that she wouldn't go and talk in a cafe but directed me to a crumbling wall opposite the factory. There, half turned away from me, she could keep one eye trained on the factory gate.

"In August," she began, "one of the lads was fooling about between jobs, so the manager gave him a tray to finish in an hour. The boy was very upset because he knew what it meant. How could he finish a whole tray in an hour? He knew at the end of the hour he would be called to the manager's office, the door would be closed, he would be sworn at and dismissed. So it happened, and when he left the factory four of his friends walked out with him."

Mrs Desai worked on that night. She knew it was wrong to spring compulsory overtime on workers five minutes before they knocked off but she was always ready to work. She began packing up at 6.55, as she always did, but was unprepared for what happened next. The supervisor shouted at her for finishing before 7.00 and when she protested she too found herself in the manager's office.

By this time, however, she had decided not to be sacked, like the others, behind a closed door. As soon as the manager became abusive she pulled open the office door and told the workers outside: "Listen to this. What is happening to me today will happen to you tomorrow. This man wouldn't speak to white workers like he speaks to us. He said he is giving me the sack, but I am leaving myself. I do not want to be given his sack."

When she walked out her son followed, but not before she had given the manager this prophetic warning:

"What you are running is not a factory but a zoo. But in a zoo there are many types of animals. Some are monkeys who dance on your fingertips. But some are lions who can bite your head off. We are those lions, Mr Manager."

Once outside, Mrs Desai organised the other five. "I told them we must act together. We must meet outside the factory on the Monday morning. I told them that I had heard my husband talk about something called "union" but what it was I was not sure."

On Monday, she resolved she would send her son on his bike to the Citizens' Advice Bureau to find out what this "union" meant. Her son was advised to visit the Brent Law Centre. There he would find a man called Jack Dromey, who knew the names of one or two unions. By the end of the week they had 200 workers out. On the eighth day APEX made the strike official.

Management reacted ferociously. They refused to meet APEX and refused government mediation through the Advisory Conciliation and Arbitration Service. They wrote offensive letters to Pavitt and Freeson, the two Labour MPs. They openly drew up a blacklist, filming marchers and pickets.

Directors abused the picket line with foul language and drove their cars through at speed. One director knocked a girl down. Another ran over Mrs Desai, and his car had to be reversed off her foot. The police, who have arrested several pickets, have felt unable so far to formulate charges against the directors.

The verbal intimidation reveals the racist and sexist psychology of the Grunwick management. Remarks are made to workers about the sex life of women on the picket line. One manager leered at Mrs Desai: "You can't win with that sari on. Why don't you change into a mini-skirt?"

Mrs Desai never lets abuse pass. "I'll tell you something manager," she said. "Mrs Gandhi wears a sari and she runs a country of 600 million people. You can't even run a little factory. Compared to her you are nothing."

Mrs Desai wants it stressed that management tried to degrade all women in this way, not just her. And the women hit back collectively, in deeds. With the help of Brent Trades Council they organised a petition signed by 6,500 people in four days, a national blacking of Grunwick and its subsidiaries (Cooper and Pearson, Bonuspool and Truecolour) and a highly successful fund-raising tour of local factories.

The Grunwick directors seem unable to grasp that their crude tactics serve only to toughen the resistance of the women. Their latest blunder is to offer a 15 per cent wage increase if those still working vote "no" in the ACAS ballot, while threatening that anyone voting "yes" will get the sack. However, my impression is that their biggest mistake was that day on August 21 when they victimised not another "monkey" in a sari but a determined "lioness" who has been mauling them now solidly for the past 12 weeks.

He fought... and he died

Mario Rodriguez, exclusive interview

San Salvador's Catholic archbishop, who has braved death threats in his fight for human rights, was gunned down at his altar on Monday night as he prepared to say mass.

Gunmen opened fire on Archbishop Oscar Arnulfo Romero with machine-guns just before the start of a service in the chapel of the Divine Providence hospital in the western suburb of this violent city.

The 63-year-old prelate, who was taken to the main hospital by nuns, was nominated last year by a group of British MPs for the Nobel Peace Prize.

Just before his death, San Salvador's archbishop of only two years said: "Christians are not afraid to fight. They are capable of fighting but prefer to speak the language of peace."

Deeply concerned by the spiral of uncontainable violence, the spiritual guide of the Salvadoran Catholics stressed that the "common enemy of our people is the oligarchy – that is, the 14 families - increasingly insatiable, and to whom I shout this warning: open your hands, give your rings, because the time will come when you have your hands cut off!"

A man of the people, simple and modest, Monsignor Romero had unreservedly up to his death defended the interests of the dispossessed, whom he urged to better their organisation "to fight effectively for an authentic society, with social justice and freedom."

Romero had turned his Sunday Mass in the cathedral of San Salvador into a centre of political attention for worshippers, the national and overseas press and, of course, for those who never

---

This interview with the champion of liberation theology Archbishop Romero was conducted exclusively for the Morning Star by the Prensa Latina news agency journalist Mario Rodriguez. It appeared on the day when news broke of the archbishop's assassination.

attended but always heard about his messages: those who are responsible for the violence.

So the killings, disappearances, arbitrary arrests, torture, acts of terrorism, that is, all that attacks human dignity, was denounced each week by this Caton of a church which realises that changes will come with or without it, but which, by its very nature, must be committed to the Salvadoran people's efforts to attain social liberation.

This "voice of the voiceless" rang out clear and precise: it accused the criminals by their full names. And recently from the pulpit of the cathedral, Monsignor Romero had demanded the resignation of none other than Col. Jose Guillermo Garcia, the key man in the first, and in the current, ruling junta, its Minister of Defence and Public Security.

Even before Monday's assassination he had already been the victim of several attacks on his life, which he referred to as "crowns of thorns, at times very hard," but about which he would rather not speak.

A priest since the age of 38, Oscar Arnulfo Romero had recently received two European prizes that offer an eloquent demonstration of international solidarity with his work as "pillar of the truth" in a country where a corrupt press has forced the people to express themselves on the rocks of the fields and the walls of the buildings.

In his home in the oncological Hospital of the Divine Providence, far from his native "Ciudad Barrios," the eastern part of the country, the archbishop made an exception just before his death and granted us an exclusive interview. He said:

"The cause of all our ills is the oligarchy, that handful of families who care nothing for the hunger of the people but who need that hunger to be able to have available cheap, abundant labour to raise and export their crops.

"The national and foreign-owned industrial companies base their ability to compete on the international market on starvation wages. It explains the all-out opposition to any kind of reform or union organising designed to improve our living standards.

"And repression against the people becomes, for that handful of families, a necessity for maintaining and increasing their profit levels, at the cost of the growing poverty of the working classes.

"Now, wealth and property bring political, economic and social power, without which it is impossible to maintain privileges, even at the cost of human dignity itself.

"The armed forces are in charge of protecting the interests of the oligarchy, of guarding the economic and political structure with the pretext that it is the national interest and security. All those who are not in agreement with the state are declared enemies of the nation and the most execrable acts are justified as requirements for national security.

"Everything here is geared to the interests of the oligarchy, an all-powerful group, that feels utter scorn for the people and their rights.

"In my third pastoral letter I defended the right of workers to organise, and in the name of the gospel, I pledged to support all that is just in their demands and denounce all attempts to destroy them.

"Now, in the country's present situation, I believe more than ever in the mass organisations; I believe in the real need of the Salvadoran people to organise, because I believe that the mass organisations are the social forces that will wield pressure, that will push toward an authentic society, with social justice and liberty.

"In politics my role is that of shepherd: to orient, guide, point to more efficient objectives. And because I esteem the mass organisations, I feel a great satisfaction with the spirit of unity, which is coming about in actual practice. The commonweal must be saved by all of us together.

"I've reached the conclusion that the situation of social justice is so grave, it has reached a stage at which faith itself has been perverted, transformed into a crime to defend economic, material interests.

"A state of perversion has been reached, with the extreme of torturing and murdering. The victims have been most precisely those most committed to the liberation of the Salvadoran people.

"Priests called for change, they promoted it, and they organised workers and peasants, but the oligarchy oppose all changes, all organisation; they do not want to hear the words agrarian reform, or anything else that would mean even the slightest modification of the present situation.

"Those exemplary priests, worthy of all respect and admiration, were victims of a desire to preserve an unjust order.

"Barreta Moto, Rutilio Grande, Navarro Oviedo, Ortiz and others were farsighted. They perceived reality with total clarity and declared that the common enemy of our people is the oligarchy. They died for it.

"The church must confront an environment of lies and lack of sincerity, where truth itself is enslaved to the interest of wealth and power.

"Human exploitation must be denounced; discrimination, violence inflicted upon human beings, upon the people, their conscience and their convictions.

"The church must accompany the people in their fight for liberation. An authentic church is duty bound to stand with and among the poor, in solidarity with their risks and their fate as victims of persecution; the church must stand ready to bear supreme witness of its love to defend those whom Jesus loved above all others.

"That is my aim, and I ask God to help me to be strong enough because I fear the weakness of the flesh. At difficult times we are all afraid; the instinct of self-preservation is very strong.

"And that is why I ask for help; help not only for myself but for all those who are engaged in this pastoral work; help to remain in our posts, because we have a great deal to do even though it be only to gather dead bodies and absolve the dying.

"The flame of social justice must always remain alive in the heart of the Salvadoran people."

Morning Star, Tuesday 16 October 1984

The women of Kent are not for turning

David Whitfield

Lynn Brown's boot thumped into the side of the "scab wagon." Her face up to the meshed window of the transit and her fists clenched tight, Lynn howled abuse at the cringing shadowy wretches in their cage.

Other women and children jostled round echoing Lynn's insults and jibes as the scab guards in blue fell out of four vans to hustle them away from the wagon's rear door.

Across a patch of grass the scab's wife, cradling a crying baby, stood outside her front door watching on as the women in the middle of the street jabbed the air with their fingers and chanted "scab, scab." The police bodily bounced them down the road.

An elderly veteran pit worker hoarsely shouted his challenge to settle it there and then as a police giant towered over him.

Out from the arse-end of the scab wagon the round-shouldered strikebreaker scurried across the grass like a scolded dog. His head low, staring at the mud and chin digging into his chest, he hunched his shoulders up as if he could hide.

Pushing the woman and child into the old coal board house he quickly turned. He looked mean and shameless. A quick V-sign and he was gone, to spend a long night in guarded isolation. His self-imposed curfew started just after 4pm.

As the scab convoy moved off, his collaborators, safe behind their

---

This feature appeared midway through the year-long miners' strike of 1984-85 against the Tories' massacre of the coalfields. David Whitfield was deputy editor of the Morning Star from the early to late 1980s. His reports from the Occupied Territories in 1982 were published as a Morning Star pamphlet, Palestine – A Land With People.

meshed wire and more than 30-strong police escort, bravely made faces at the frustrated women.

Lynn Brown was left squaring up to one of the scab's round-the-clock guards, venting her anger at the unwelcome intruder in her village.

The top of her arm was bright pink. Crushed capillaries marked the first signs of a bruise. A young teenage girl showed the crescent of deep finger-nail prints in her forearm.

Walking back to the local miners' welfare, chairwoman of the village women's support group and pit canteen worker, Aurelia Pugh snapped, "I'd shoot them, they'll never be able to live here when we've won."

Like most others in Elvington she believes the scabs have been given coal board guarantees of new lives when the miners win.

Neither Lynn nor Aurelia would have said boo to a goose eight months ago say neighbours.

In the small village of Elvington in Kent the strikebreaker, Brian Wright, is a hated man.

The men point out he's never in his life been down the shaft, like most of the 15 or so going into the local Tilmanstone pit. "He don't know the colour of coal." And the women recall the day he evicted his teenage pregnant daughter.

She was taken in by a mining family now on strike.

Just before he crawled to the coal board and the Tories, scab Brian Wright took daughter and child back. Today he hides behind the innocent screaming infant, brandishing it like a shield at his windows before the striking demonstrators.

His other party trick is to wave his wage dockets. It makes his police friends giggle.

Before the miners' strike Elvington was a quiet pit village. There was no crime and the children were polite to the local bobby.

Today there is no local bobby.

Instead van loads of unwelcome police bring their riot gear from as far away as Dorset, Sussex and Cambridgeshire as well as the capital.

Younger children are now frightened to go to school past the frequent police picket and their questions: "Is your daddy a picket?" The older children are sullen, hostile and ready with lip.

'It's all been done in broad daylight," explains Lesley Ives, secretary of the support group. "As the kids have gone to the post office to get sweets they've seen their dads dragged across the road."

Margaret Halford, miners' welfare caretaker, adds: "The kids are heartbroken, they hate the police."

At the beginning of last month the police put Elvington under siege. The plan was to intimidate the 70 or so mining families.

Mining families standing in their own front gardens were ordered indoors. Others on the streets, including one local farmworker out buying a loaf, were arbitrarily arrested.

Young girls in their early teens were told they'd be picked up for soliciting.

Boys like Ken Pugh, 17, and one of only nine lucky lads taken on in the pit's latest recruiting drive, were beaten where it wouldn't show – and even bitten. "He wouldn't tell me, his mother, some of the things they did to him," says Aurelia.

A mobile lock-up was parked in the village as the police tried to impose a curfew.

But when strikebreaker Alan Beer fired his 12-bore shot-gun over the heads of 16 women, men and children – including Aurelia Pugh – out walking to keep the village open, the police response was to threaten them all with the 1875 Conspiracy and Protection of Property Act for "watching and besetting a house without lawful authority."

Today, the Elvington mining community is united, unintimidated and still walking the streets – unlike the scabs. The women's support group ended its meeting last week with a silent 10-minute vigil across the road from the scab's house to emphasise the point.

"We're not frightened of them any more," says self-confessed beset-ter Aurelia Pugh with contempt.

In the union office it is the women's support group banner which hangs on the wall. It is a justified mark of respect.

Along with the men of Elvington they are fighting to save some 830 jobs at Tilmanstone. It's an all-consuming task and Aurelia jokes that her husband, Jack, a militant member of the pit deputies' union NACODS, is sueing the NUM for divorce – "citing 900 men," she laughs.

Although Tilmanstone and neighbouring pit Snowdown – which the board has admitted it wants shut – are sitting on an untapped seam with an estimated 50-year life, there are strong fears the whole Kent coalfield is threatened with closure.

Till the late '60s Elvington was entirely a pit village. Then the local council took over the coal board houses and now about a third of the 1,200 population are connected with the pit.

But the union owns the local club, empty last week except for the women's group meeting. It also owns the children's playground, the football pitches, bowling green and the doctor's surgery.

If the pit goes, this corner of Kent to the north of Dover will become a de-industrialised unemployment desert. Communities like Elvington will be replaced by commuting stock-brokers.

The determined resistance to the closure plan has called for great sacrifices.

"I've worked since my son was 18 months old," says Lynn. "I've always planned and budgeted, but now I'm penniless."

Her husband, Dave, is a striking faceworker. Like many other women in the village she is working as a farm labourer to make ends meet.

Lesley Ives sold her caravan and watched a neighbour take her own children, not Lesley's, on holiday. As she adds: "We've got nothing left to lose."

But for some women like Jean Powell and Joan Brown the going has been particularly rough.

They both work at the pit in the canteen, are members of the NUM, and are on strike. So are their husbands, Norris and George.

For eight months they have had no income whatsoever. They have lived off food parcels.

Jean's big night out is a lemonade at the women's support group meeting. Joan's daughter keeps her in cigarettes and her son Andrew has paid most of the bills.

"We cropped the garden this year," says Joan, "so that's come in very handy. You can make a meal on vegetables, though I've never before gone without meat on a Sunday."

Jean and Joan go picketing most days – "We do our duty" – but Jean admits it's tiring and depressing worrying every day how to eke out the food parcels to get one main meal. Her dream of a new stair-carpet burst months ago.

"One day your morale is up, another it is down," she says, frankly adding, "it's miserable – you just have to put a brave face on everything. If you didn't you'd go doo lalley."

With her brother-in-law a scab, life is not made any easier for Jean and Norris, a development ripper. Her in-laws are against the strike.

"You'd think I was the scab," she says bitterly.

Aurelia explains the women's support group is vital and not just for food. "We keep each other going." She explains: "If one of us needs a moan then they can moan to us.

"What cash is lacking we make up for in community spirit."

And when the strike is over that support will still be vital.

"These women will still have two or three years' hardship before they pull themselves up after this," she adds. But with all the understandable difficulties going back is out of the question.

"These are the sort of people," explains Aurelia, "Thatcher thought wouldn't come up trumps for Arthur Scargill. Well, they're not fighting for Arthur Scargill, they're fighting for themselves.

"Arthur Scargill," says Aurelia, who thinks he's a hero, "is fighting for what we know we want. We're the ones who will tell Arthur when we go back – when we've won everything.

"This strike won't break till we say so."

And Lynn Brown adds: "When this strike is over it won't end there. What we've been given has got to be returned, paid back."

The meek and mild of eight months ago are now committing themselves to a working-class struggle which must continue in support of other workers' demands.

So, last week, as the women's support group served over 50 strikers' children with a dinner of mashed spuds – the best part of a hundredweight – meat loaf and cabbage followed by Angel Whirl, Aurelia Pugh spoke for them all:

"Thatcher says a year, we'll give her two or three if she likes.

"We've won," she stated, "we're just waiting for Thatcher to admit it.

"She thinks she's the iron lady, well, she's met nothing yet – the women of Kent are not for turning."

Morning Star, Tuesday 4 February 1986

Murdoch caught redhanded

Mick Costello

Rupert Murdoch's vicious plans for his war on the unions have fallen into the hands of the Morning Star.

They reveal that months of careful scheming went into his callous sacking of 5,000 printworkers after he had provoked a strike on the Sun, Times, News of the World and Sunday Times.

According to a secret document from legal advisers Farrer and Co, the main consideration in the minds of News International bosses was how to find the right moment when workers could be sacked without any compensation.

Mr Geoffrey Richards, for the lawyers, reminds Mr Murdoch's managing director Bruce Matthews: "We talked about this some months ago."

The document is dated December 20, 1985. It advises Mr Matthews, who is also Mr Murdoch's chief negotiator with the unions, to sack all the workers while they are on strike if he wants to save money on them.

The legal advice was of such importance that copies of it also went to Mr Murdoch and Bill O'Neill (his main hatchetman) and six other News International chieftains.

It opens with the statement: "If the moment came when it was necessary to dispense with the current workforces of TNL and NGN, the cheapest way of doing so would be to dismiss employees while participating in a strike or other industrial action.

Mick Costello's exposure of Rupert Murdoch's union-busting battle plan appeared just a couple of weeks into the year-long Wapping strike, provoked by the sacking of 5,000 workers when his companies transferred operations to London's Docklands.

"A strike would be better because it would be easier to identify a striker."

TNL publishes The Times and Sunday Times, and NGN publishes the Sun and News of the World.

It then lists what it calls "the advantages" of sacking a striker, explaining that "helpfully," however, the courts tend to interpret "other industrial action" in a very broad sense.

Workers must be dismissed while they are actually on strike. The lawyers say: "That may be a difficulty for us, not least because of the large numbers involved."

They express the hope that an office branch committee decision to strike will be taken by an industrial tribunal to mean that "each and every member" has taken the action.

In cool and calculating fashion special consideration is given to how to get rid of "sick employees" and "frightened employees" (that is those who stay away from work because they do not want to cross picket lines).

It says: "There may be merit in having piles of dismissal letters at exit doors, even if that involves an element of duplication. We talked about this some months ago."

It examines how best to cover workers on all shifts and in the many departments.

The advice is then clear: "The idea is to catch as many employees in the net as possible, and it seems to me likely that that will be done best if the dismissals take place at the weekend."

On December 29 Mr Murdoch forced a strike when he announced that he was going ahead with using his new presses at Wapping without any agreement with the print unions. The strike recommendation was agreed on January 11 by the unions.

All attempts at mediation, by the Advisory, Conciliation and Arbitration Service and by the TUC's general secretary Norman Willis were rejected by Mr Murdoch.

He snubbed the unions after they had secured a "Yes" for action, and as the strike began on January 24, sacked the workforce at the Central London presses, moving their work to Wapping, East London.

The secret document shows that Mr Murdoch was following the

lawyers' advice. They advise that no worker will have a claim "in unfair dismissal, provided all strikers have been dismissed and none selectively re-engaged."

The December 20 brief from his lawyers admits: "Given that we are now much nearer the date of a possible explosion," it would be "sensible" to go over the advice that had already been thoroughly looked at on previous occasions.

Who's afraid of Boris Yeltsin?

Fred Weir in Moscow

Boris Yeltsin is running for president. In the turmoil and gloom that characterise Soviet politics today, the Russian republican leader, who seems driven by negative energy, is the man of the hour.

Mr Yeltsin, a former career Communist Party apparatchik, is riding high in virtually all public opinion polls, while Soviet President Mikhail Gorbachov has sunk to an all-time low.

Mr Yeltsin is now also being described as "the man with the plan," because of his programmatic statement read out last week at an emergency session of the Russian Congress of Peoples' Deputies.

There is a pervasive sense here, helped along by serious errors on the part of the central government, that things are building to some sort of final showdown between Yeltsin and Gorbachov.

That may be illusory, but Boris Yeltsin's current popularity is not. Unlike his circle of "radical" intellectual advisers, Mr Yeltsin is able to relate and communicate with working people. His base of support is the USSR's most concentrated industrial city, Sverdlovsk, which he ran as party secretary for many years.

In his recent climb up the ladder of electoral politics, he has been tremendously successful at dramatising his political battles as personal ones, crusading first against Yegor Ligachov and now against Gorbachov himself.

Mr Yeltsin won the presidency of the huge Russian republic last spring by a very narrow margin in the Russian Congress of Peoples'

The Canadian journalist Fred Weir reported for the Morning Star from Moscow throughout the 1990s. This article appeared some four months before the abortive August coup which propelled Boris Yeltsin to power.

Deputies. He has used that as his base in a power struggle with the central government which is now threatening to fly out of control.

The issues are real: Division of property, power and prerogative. But Mr Yeltsin's penchant for macho rivalry has helped to turn it into a dangerous confrontation between himself and the Soviet president.

Last month both won political victories. The March 17 referendum carried overwhelmingly in favour of Mr Gorbachov's vision for a new type of federation – the final results released last week showed 76.4 per cent of those who voted in the entire country backed unity. In the Russian republic, more than 71 per cent voted "yes," a slap in the face to Mr Yeltsin's "radical" supporters who had urged people to cast negative ballots.

Boris Yeltsin can claim an equally resounding win. Almost 70 per cent of Russian voters supported his idea of a popularly elected Russian presidency. The only credible candidate for the post at this moment would be Yeltsin himself.

The position would enable him to manoeuvre independently of the parliament which now elects and controls the president.

Under the surface, however, things are not going all that well for Mr Yeltsin.

In February he faced rebellion in his own ranks when six of his top deputies accused him, in a public statement, of a political style marked by "authoritarianism, confrontation and a tendency to take individual decisions on matters of domestic and foreign policy in disregard of the law and the opinion of constitutional bodies.

"Though he promised to promote the unity of society, he has led the (Russian) parliament and republic into a fierce confrontation between political forces," the rebels said.

Though Mr Yeltsin has rhetorically championed independence from the USSR for Russia, the Baltic states and others, he has himself become embroiled in bickering and ham-handed manoeuvres against the autonomy of Russia's own numerous national minorities.

Just how badly he has alienated them became clear last week when the Soviet news agency TASS reported that 14 out of 16 autonomous republics within the Russian federation and five out six autonomous regions refused even to distribute ballots on their territory for the

"Yeltsin" question on March 17, while all of them voted in overwhelming majorities for the union.

Relations with Russia's ethnic minorities took a turn for the worse after Mr Yeltsin met on March 23 with Georgia's ultra-nationalist leader Zviad Gamsakhurdia and signed a protocol dismissing the minority South Ossetian territory of Georgia as a "former autonomous region."

Last year the Georgian parliament, in defiance of the Soviet constitution, dissolved the autonomous status of South Ossetia, and, by all accounts, the Georgian government has since carried out a campaign of physical terror against the territory's culturally Islamic inhabitants. Fifty people have died in the past three months.

Mr Yeltsin's apparent support for the Georgian leader's chauvinist and ethnic purity policies comes as dynamite for Russia's diverse ethnic population.

Last week the USSR Supreme Soviet finally declared a state of emergency in South Ossetia, and sent in troops to protect the region's population from Georgian intimidation.

Another question mark for Boris Yeltsin is how long his alliance-of-convenience with the "liberal" intelligentsia of Moscow and Leningrad will hold out.

Most "radicals" have long since abandoned Mikhail Gorbachov in disappointment over his failure to bring in sweeping free-market reform and carry the political process into an East European-style clean sweep of the Communist Party and Socialist institutions.

Many of the leading lights of perestroika have now flocked to the Yeltsin banner, and his "brain trust" boasts such names as sociologist Tatiana Zaslavskaya, Americanologist Georgi Arbatov and historian Dmitri Volkonogov.

Yet there remains open contempt among the intelligentsia for Mr Yeltsin's rough-hewn ways, his provincial accent and his "populist" political style. They envy his ability to mobilise the masses, and fear it in equal measure.

On a visit to Japan last month, "radical" Moscow mayor Gavril Popov spoke in dreamy terms of Mr Yeltsin as the "battering ram" that will knock down the gates of power on behalf of the "genuine democrats," who will walk through them.

Similarly Nikolai Travkin, leader of the "radical" Democratic Party, told a Leningrad newspaper that Mr Yeltsin is merely a "transitional figure," useful for the "democrats" only in the short run.

In fact there are considerable grounds for concern about Mr Yeltsin's demagogic style.

On March 7 he entered the October Theatre in downtown Moscow and gave the most inflammatory speech of his career to a crowd of wild supporters.

He urged them to "declare war on the country's leadership." He lashed out at "enemies" all around, and even at "traitors within the democratic camp."

He said: "A critical moment has come in the battle against the system, which is fighting for its life and will not give up the levers of power. This will be a decisive year. It will go one way or the other."

He warned that he had a "list" of local Soviet leaders that he intended to deal with and replace with "reliable men who will carry out our policies."

Mr Yeltsin later apologised in a question-and-answer session with the newspaper Komsomolskaya Pravda for those remarks, saying, incredibly, that he had put aside the prepared text of his speech once he sensed the enthusiasm of the crowd, and had spoken to them "from the heart."

Very often when Mr Yeltsin speaks one wonders whether the dog is wagging the tail, or the other way around.

However, at the emergency Congress of Peoples' Deputies last week, he mounted the podium and gave a speech read ponderously but carefully from a text prepared by his advisers.

In it he charged that the country has been deceived by President Gorbachov for six years and that perestroika "has not been restructuring but rather the last stage of the stagnation period."

Pointing to the failure of the central government to "muster the courage for radical economic reform," Mr Yeltsin proposed his own measures to stabilise the rouble, introduce market structures, grant independence to enterprises, privatise many businesses and introduce land reform.

He called for the "de-ideologisation of all state structures," much deeper demilitarisation and "non-interference in the internal affairs and life of various ethnic communities" of Russia.

He proposed dissolution of the present central government and its replacement with a broadly based democratic coalition of parties and workers' movements, including progressive-minded members of the Communist Party. Mr Yeltsin reiterated his call for a loose confederation of Soviet republics in what he termed "a federal voluntary union of equal nations."

That speech was undeniably the best of his career, and has heightened the impression all around that he is a rising star.

Despite some severe problems that Mr Gorbachov would have with several of its points, the indications are there is also much that might serve as a basis of compromise and negotiation should the two finally decide to go that route.

Mr Gorbachov too is expected to put forward an anti-crisis programme in the near future. But for the moment he appears to be drifting, increasingly isolated and under intense pressure from the Yeltsin steamroller.

Break the silence

John Haylett

Fourteen political and military leaders in Grenada have had their appeals against sentence of death rejected, yet scarcely a mention has been made of the case in the British media.

At a time when satellites orbit the planet and distance is no problem for live reports, why is there a news blackout?

Why have the major international news agencies, which carry daily reports of real or alleged breaches of human rights in the most inaccessible parts of the world united in non-coverage of the Maurice Bishop murder trial appeal?

The inescapable answer is that they are under no illusion that what has taken place in a special courthouse in Richmond Hill Prison is one of the most grotesque miscarriages of justice ever perpetrated.

Further, they understand that the entire pseudo-legal farce was planned, organised and financed by the US in the wake of its illegal invasion of Grenada on October 25 1983.

The Maurice Bishop case was conceived by the Ronald Reagan regime as a political lesson to all left-wing parties and to the people of the Caribbean that nothing would be permitted in its backyard which did not meet its approval.

US hostility to the Grenada revolution had been open since the overthrow of Washington's thuggish surrogate Eric Gairy by members of the New Jewel Movement on March 13, 1979.

The Reagan administration accused the popularly acclaimed

The Morning Star's role in publicising the plans for the judicial murder of the Grenadian revolutionary leaders almost certainly saved their lives, by breaking the media blackout not just in Britain but abroad.

John Haylett, then the paper's deputy editor, has edited the Morning Star since 1995.

People's Revolutionary Government of becoming a Soviet-Cuban military base and of exporting subversion to other Caribbean states.

A new international airport at Point Salines, which was designed to help tourism was slated as a Soviet airbase by Washington.

The US opposed international loans and assistance to Grenada, masterminded a negative propaganda war against the island and set up terror groups, one of which slaughtered three young women, when a bomb intended to wipe out the revolutionary leadership exploded during a rally in Queen's Park.

The Pentagon also organised invasion rehearsals, such as the Amber and the Amberines exercise off the coast of Puerto Rico.

The title was a play on Grenada and a group of small islands, the Grenadines, which belong to neighbouring St Vincent

Maurice Bishop himself warned on several occasions from as early as 1979 that the US was planning to invade Grenada and destroy the revolution.

Ironically, it was divisions within the party and government which resulted in the killing of Maurice Bishop, the paralysis of political leadership and the traumatisation of the Grenadian people.

A decision was taken by the central committee of the New Jewel Movement to institute a "joint leadership" proposal, giving Maurice Bishop responsibility for the public face of the revolution and his deputy Bernard Coard responsibility for party organisation and development.

This was agreed by the central committee and by an aggregate meeting of party members.

It appears that Prime Minister Bishop also concurred, but after returning from a state visit to Hungary he rejected the proposal, triggering a crisis within the party.

Earlier, assiduously spread rumours that Bernard Coard and his wife Phyllis, who was president of the National Women's Organisation, planned to murder Maurice Bishop had begun to do the rounds.

In response, and to confound the rumours, Bernard Coard resigned.

Responsibility for spreading these rumours was admitted by one Cletus St Paul, one of Maurice Bishop's bodyguards. His arrest, agreed by the Prime Minister, was ordered by the central committee.

He was later freed by US troops and was to become the key witness at the trial of the revolutionary leaders.

Events then went rapidly downhill, with the central committee detaining the PM under house arrest on October 13, while negotiations took place between government ministers and party leaders.

On the morning of October 19, a thousands-strong crowd went to the prime minister's house and freed him without opposition from armed guards.

The throng made its way to army headquarters at Fort Rupert, where soldiers present were disarmed.

Three armoured cars and a troop lorry under the command of Officer Cadet Conrad Mayers were then sent by acting head of the army Colonel Ewart Layne to restore military order at the fort.

Coming under fire – as a result of which OC Mayers was killed – the convoy used its superior firepower to retake the fort.

Civilians were ordered from the fort, with the exception of Maurice Bishop and his seven colleagues, who were summarily executed.

Army officers then set up a Revolutionary Military Committee to run the country until a new civilian government could be sworn in within a fortnight, but this never took place.

US invasion plans were given the go-ahead to attack on October 25 and despite heroic resistance by units of the People's Revolutionary Army and by Cuban construction workers, who were engaged on completing the airport, the island was in the aggressors' hands in a few days.

Over 100 Grenadians were killed, including patients at the mental hospital which was bombed, along with 24 Cubans and a number of US invaders.

Hundreds of government supporters and People's Revolutionary Army soldiers were rounded up, detained and interrogated.

The US then announced that it would put the surviving political and military leadership on trial for the murder of Maurice Bishop and seven other people.

What followed was a legal farrago, which in any law-governed state should have ensured the release of all defendants, but which, in an island under the military, financial and political control of the US and eight of its regional clients, led finally to a jury finding 17 people guilty on 196 charges in less than three hours – less than a minute per count!

The main basis for the convictions was confessions, which were tortured out of the accused and which were totally repudiated in open court.

The quality of the confessions can be gauged best by that of Major Chris Stroude, whose "evidence" implicated New Jewel Movement central committee member Chris de Riggs in a supposed meeting of the committee on October 19.

Only after Chris de Riggs had spent several months in jail did the occupying forces have to accept that this was an impossibility, since he had been off the island at the time.

Despite this, the court ruled that the confessions had been given willingly.

The judge similarly refused to accept medical evidence of torture or even to read medical records. His theory was that damage to prisoners was self-inflicted.

Even when Colonel Liam James complained of being dragged along the ground by a sock tied around his genitalia, the judge merely asked the doctor if the marks left could have been caused by masturbation – a suggestion rejected by the doctor.

Apart from the confessions, the prosecution case rested on Cletus St Paul, Maurice Bishop's former bodyguard, who gave three contradictory accounts of the events of October 19 in pre-trial hearings and at the trial.

The contradictions were such that appeal court president JOF Haynes ordered that he return to the appeal court to be re-examined.

Unfortunately, after Judge Haynes died in the middle of the appeal, his replacement Sir Frederick Smith dropped the order. St Paul's testimony was allowed to stand.

Of the original 19 defendants, army cook Fabian Gabriel, who was tortured in 1984 agreed in April 1986 to turn Queen's evidence in return for immunity from prosecution.

He obliged by identifying all eight accused People's Revolutionary Army soldiers at Fort Rupert as having been present at the shooting of Maurice Bishop, either as firing squad members or giving orders.

Another witness, fire service Inspector Williams, had earlier testified that one of the eight – Major Chris Stroude – had been elsewhere in the fort at the time, but his testimony was ignored.

Apart from the paucity of evidence against the defendants – especially the non-military members of the political leadership – the conduct of the trial was without precedent.

Empanelment of jurors was totally at variance with Grenadian law.

Jurors were allowed to curse and abuse the accused and to howl with laughter during descriptions of torture without rebuke by the trial judge.

The trial judge was engaged on a temporary basis to hear just the Maurice Bishop case.

The judge refused to stay the trial proceedings pending an Appeal Court decision on the various defence motions seeking a free and fair trial in a constitutional court.

All the male defendants had their heads shaved convict-style against their will to humiliate them and to enhance the aura of guilt about them.

The judge's summing-up was based on the prosecution's notes, since no official stenographer was in court during the prosecution case.

When the defendants chose not to co-operate with what they described as a kangaroo court, their lawyers were cited for contempt and they were refused leave to read or hear testimony against them.

Their lawyers, all eminent barristers from Jamaica and Guyana, presented 38 legal submissions to the Appeal Court relating to the unconstitutionality of the court and the illegality of its proceedings.

All were dismissed in jig time, with little effort to answer the legal basis of the submissions.

International human rights lawyers of the calibre of Lord Tony Gifford, trade union bodies in Britain and France and many individuals have already written to Grenada's Prime Minister Nicholas Brathwaite expressing their misgivings over the court verdicts.

Execution of these 14 people will benefit only the US. It will set back the process of reconciliation in Grenada.

Morning Star, Friday 2 August 1991

Grenadian ministers hide from media

John Haylett

Grenada's beleaguered lynch-mob ministers yesterday cut themselves off from telephone and fax contacts with the outside world in a bid to avoid embarrassing questions over the regime's plans for a spate of political hangings.

Fax machines to Governor-General Sir Paul Scoon and Prime Minister Sir Nicholas Brathwaite's offices were disconnected, while staff in ministerial offices were under orders not to put calls through to their ministers.

Sir Paul, who is the Queen's representative in Grenada, the prime minister and two other key ministers Dr Francis Alexis and Joan Purcell have been permanently "at a meeting" over recent days.

Both Dr Alexis and Ms Purcell sit on the so-called Mercy Committee, which recommended over a week ago to the governor-general that five out of 14 people who were sentenced to death for the murder of former Prime Minister Maurice Bishop should be hanged.

Because of a defence motion served on the Attorney-General late on Sunday night, the hangings scheduled for Tuesday morning were postponed, yet the names of the five men were not released to either their families or to the media.

Asked for the identity of the five men yesterday, Ms Purcell's secretary told the Morning Star: "I have no information on that.

"You just have to go ahead with whatever information our information office gives you," she added, perhaps unaware that the information office had none to give.

The governor-general's secretary was "not aware" that the mercy committee had provided him with the names of those recommended for hanging. "I don't know much about that part of things," she said.

Supreme Court Registrar Sandra Belfon confirmed that the Court of Appeal, which will sit in judgement next Wednesday on the appeal motion submitted by the defence lawyer Clarence Hughes, will consist of the same judges who dismissed the 14 people's extensive and substantial appeals three weeks ago.

Ms Belfon also professed total ignorance of which five defendants had been due to be hanged on Tuesday.

"I do not have this information, sir. When a final decision would have been made, as registrar of the court, I would have been told. I was not told officially anything.

"There are certain officials who must be told when the executions are going to take place. They're the persons who must be there. I would have to be told beforehand," she said.

However, when asked about the hangings set for Tuesday, Ms Belfon added: "That's what I understand, but I was not advised officially of that.

"I was advised that I would be told when the time came," but she had no idea how much notice she would be given of such an event.

At the Attorney-General's office, which Ms Belfon recommended for further information, the stonewall treatment was just as effective, if less sophisticated.

After recommending that the aforementioned Ms Belfon was the person to try, Dr Alexis's secretary said: "Hold on," before cutting the Star off on successive calls.

"This cover-up by Grenadian ministers is very worrying," said Jean Tate of the Committee for Human Rights in Grenada last night in London. "It shows that they have a lot to hide.

"How can all of these people at the heart of things claim not to even know who is due to be hanged, when the gallows has already been prepared, the men measured for execution suits and hoods and the graves dug?" she asked.

"Clearly the government wants the Court of Appeal to dismiss Clarence Hughes's motion out of hand on Wednesday and then to push ahead with the hangings on Thursday.

"Pressure must be stepped up on the Grenada authorities and the US government, which still calls the shots in Grenada.

"The Foreign and Commonwealth Office must also be pressured to intervene to ensure that these people get their right to appeal to the Privy Council in London, the highest court in the Commonwealth."

Ms Tate called for a mass turnout from 6pm until midnight on Tuesday, August 6, outside the Privy Council offices in Whitehall near Downing Street. A further vigil will take place the following day from noon until 1pm.

Biting on the bullet

John Haylett interview with Chris Hani

Anyone suggesting in the 1980s that, by August 1991, the South African Communist Party would be legal and its Soviet counterpart illegal would have been seen as a suitable case for treatment.

But it happened – and it meant that the newly legalised SACP and its African National Congress allies have had to operate in an international and domestic situation far different from that envisaged during their struggle against the apartheid regime.

Communist leader Chris Hani, who is also a national executive committee member of the ANC, is in no doubt that the movement has a lot to learn.

"Our approach must be to create a popular democracy – an accountable society," he stresses.

"We must look at our history critically and remove the blinkers that we all wore. We mustn't feel that it is disloyal to criticise.

"We made the mistake of accepting the Soviet Union as a model in all circumstances. If communists in the Soviet Union had dared to criticise, I believe that socialism there would be still alive and kicking today," he insists.

"We have broad agreement within the ANC because of the organisation's democratic open style.

"Democracy for us is not democracy for the elites. The ANC negotiating commission will report back to a working committee, which will consult with the SACP and COSATU and will then call in regional leaders to discuss the issues.

"It means that there are sharp discussions, even heated debate, but we manage to bring everyone along," he explains.

This interview with the South African Communist Party general secretary Chris Hani appeared just weeks before he was murdered by an apartheid assassin at Easter 1993.

Another lesson, which Hani believes it is necessary to take in the light of the Soviet experience, is the need for a flexible approach to the economy.

While remaining firm on the need for a future ANC government to negotiate an economic reconstruction package with the party and the trade unions – to deal with poverty, jobs provision, health and education – he believes that widespread nationalisation is not feasible.

"Communists and socialists are now beginning to realise that nationalisation is not necessarily the answer to all problems of economic development," he asserts.

Nationalisation of certain areas of the public utilities will be needed to facilitate electrification, bring clean water to all South Africans and make sure that public transport is accessible to workers and poor people.

In addition, the government would take a stake in industries like mining to enable its voice to be heard and to affect economic policy.

"An ANC government's supporters would lack the skills to run industries, but this does not mean we could be held to ransom.

"Everything in the country must reflect the reality that we are doing away with the political and economic domination of the majority by the minority."

To this end, Chris Hani proposes that programmes should be set up to assist black people in acquiring management, marketing and other skills.

He also calls for an enhanced role for the trade union movement.

"The trade unions must be the watchdog at the workplace. Why should we not be pushing for decision-making at the plant by workers, who are totally involved in the work of the plant?" he asks.

This control function for the union would, he believes, militate against the kind of statist failing, common both to the British Labour and Soviet communist approaches to public ownership.

Despite his criticisms of the Soviet experience, Hani believes that it is necessary to keep a sense of balance and not to dismiss its very real achievements.

"Didn't the Soviet Union create a situation, where the oppressed countries for the first time had a shield to defend themselves against the forces of imperialism and colonialism?

"Didn't the Soviet Union assist virtually all the revolutionary struggles in the world?

"Didn't they help to boost the morale of all working-class parties in their struggles?"

"Didn't they solve the problems of illiteracy and provide services to people which Yeltsin has now withdrawn?" he asks.

"Nevertheless, the abuses, distortions, bureaucracy and absence of human rights must be attacked openly, so that never again will we commit those things in the name of socialism," he declares.

In this connection, he is optimistic about the socialist system in Cuba, from which he returned with an SACP delegation last weekend.

Accepting that the system is far from perfect, he says that Cuba has solved basic problems of education and health provision that no other Latin American country has solved – despite being subjected to a US economic blockade for over 30 years.

He believes that the Cuban leadership is closer to the people than its Soviet counterparts had been, that it encourages criticism and that there is no yawning lifestyle gap between people and leadership.

"A solidarity campaign with Cuba is now the key solidarity campaign for all progressives. The world should build up solidarity with Cuba, as we did with Vietnam," he recommends.

Turning to the ticklish questions of negotiations with the de Klerk regime and of sharing power with the National Party in a government of national unity, the communist leader says that he has "no problem" with power-sharing.

"How long will power-sharing last? The National Party wants five years or more. We want to shorten the pain of being with the NP in government.

"It's an albatross around our necks. We want, at the right time, to drop it," he stresses.

However, he is aware of the contradictory feelings besetting white South Africans – wanting change, but fearing what it may bring.

"We want this transition to be as painless as possible.

"We have seen that, in the white group, there are elements that are unhappy with developments, unhappy with the dismantling of apartheid – some are in the Civil Service, some in the security forces.

"The question is: how to prevent a rebellion to stop democracy from being fulfilled. That's why we need a limited period of a government of national unity," he explains.

There are still many question marks against the motives of apartheid President FW de Klerk, who has still done very little against those of his erstwhile supporters, who have stoked up violence – either directly against ANC supporters or indiscriminately to heighten social psychosis.

The state president could have questioned former British National Front supporter Bruce Anderson – and until his deportation a leader of Inkatha – about who was helping him to smuggle arms to the organisation.

The president didn't do so, contenting himself with expelling Anderson from the country, but then made a great song and dance about three ANC members caught bringing weapons into Natal – the Inkatha warlords' killing fields.

Although the government had four days to raise this question with the ANC, it waited until the morning of a bilateral meeting to blow it up into a major row, possibly seeking to engineer a split between the ANC and its south Natal leadership, especially veteran communist Harry Gwala.

Gwala has organised self-defence squads against the Inkatha gangs and remarked enigmatically that "when they come for us, we won't welcome them with bibles."

Chris Hani recalls that in the late '80s, Inkatha launched a reign of terror in the townships around Pietermaritzburg to wipe out ANC cadres.

"Gwala comes from a region which has suffered a lot of violence. His top lieutenants have been gunned down and eliminated.

"He lives in a situation teeming with warlords, violence and murder. A leader of his stature sees it as his responsibility to provide a measure of protection to his constituency.

"Anyone who judges Gwala must judge him as a person in this situation. Gwala wants peace – he doesn't want surrender.

"There is a dialectical connection between the struggle for peace and self-defence," Hani insists, pointing out that the development of self-defence units was a way of combating death squads, "without violating our agreements with this regime, in terms of suspending our military operations."

He identifies an element of hypocrisy in the government, since it says nothing about heavily armed neighbourhood watches in white areas to defend these rich communities against criminals, while denying black townships the right to defend themselves against attack.

"I doubt that the ANC would have any organisation in some areas of Natal, if the comrades had not gone out to acquire skills, get weapons, and defend themselves and the people," he declares.

The ongoing violence is, he believes, a reason for wasting no time in bringing forward democratic elections, since accepting the opposite argument would encourage those elements against a settlement to foment bloodshed.

The ANC has shown itself willing to compromise. It is in favour of a government of national unity, but insists on real progress toward democracy.

And this must mean, states Chris Hani, that de Klerk must stop dithering and "bite the bullet."

Morning Star, Friday 16 July 1999

The poison of Louis de Bernieres

Andrew Murray, Eyes Left

Every season has its fashionable book and, this summer, it is the novel Captain Corelli's Mandolin by Louis de Bernieres.

You can see it everywhere – there are racks of copies in all bookshops and one even found its way into Hugh Grant's hand in the last scene of Notting Hill, the film of the season.

Beware. This romantic novel, set on a Greek island during the second world war, is a work of its time in more ways than one. It is a book of the most crude and brazen anti-communism which manages, no doubt by coincidence, to also serve as an apologia for external interference in the Balkans.

My suspicions were first raised when an early chapter in the book sought to portray the Greek dictator Metaxas in a sympathetic light. The narrative then presents the Italian fascist army – the force which exterminated one-third of the population of Libya, to name but one of its crimes – as a collection of amiable and romantic buffoons, presenting no real threat to anyone.

The cause of Greek democracy was not one the Morning Star had suddenly discovered when Andrew Murray exposed the political speciousness of the novelist Louis de Bernieres in 1999. In The Story of the Daily Worker, *published 50 years before, Allen Hutt wrote: "The betrayal of liberation in Greece, for which Mr Churchill above all must bear the historic responsibility, was to present the Daily Worker with a cause and a campaign only paralleled in its history by the war in Spain."*

The paper's foreign editor Malcolm MacEwen, who reported from Greece in 1945, wrote in his memoirs The Greening of a Red: *"If I ask why I stayed with the Daily Worker until 1956 a large part of the answer lies in my experience of the British-sponsored terror in*

De Bernieres is clearly an apologist for the excesses of the right in Greece. But if every other character is painted in nuanced and sympathetic colours, the communist freedom fighters of ELAS/EAM, who fought the fascists throughout the war and for an independent Greece after it, are portrayed as dehumanised sadists and rapists without any redeeming merit.

Their contribution to the anti-fascist struggle is denied, their relationship to the Greek people traduced, their political discourse rendered ridiculous.

The only major characters in the book who could be described as left-wing speedily repent of their aberration as the plot develops.

Captain Corelli's Mandolin has, nevertheless, been praised to the skies. Reviewers have admired its plot and its handling of the main characters. The poisonous political message woven into the narrative is taken for granted, relying on the ignorance of most readers regarding the history of the period in question.

But, of course, this libelling of the left and whitewashing of the right serves a definite purpose today – by rewriting the history of the second world war to demonise the strongest anti-fascists and those who fought hardest for the independence of Greece it can only act as political prop for the new neocolonialism in the Balkans.

Whether or not that is de Bernieres's intention, I cannot say, although I would suspect he has some personal axe to grind in regard to Greek politics. What is clear is that, once again, under the guise of popular culture, a reactionary message is being spread far and wide.

Greece... Greece showed me the cynicism, hypocrisy and brutality of the Labour government's foreign policy."

Later in the 1940s, Betty Bartlett reported for the paper from Athens. She married the leader of the Greek seafarers' union Tony Ambatielos, who spent many years imprisoned by successive fascist regimes. Betty Ambatielos was herself interned after the Colonels' coup in the spring of 1967 and reported on her experiences for the Morning Star that June.

Andrew Murray worked for the Morning Star as a sub-editor and then parliamentary correspondent in the late 1970s until 1985. His Eyes Left column appeared in the paper from 1998 to 2000.

Morning Star, Wednesday 28 July 1999

Literary gent tosses off criticism

Louis de Bernieres, letter
I was delighted to receive a hostile notice from Eyes Left and so am writing to thank you for this indirect vindication.

Your ship has sunk, brothers. It was historically inevitable, and just now the historical conditions have been fulfilled. Goodbye to the biggest failure and disappointment since the non-return of Christ. How long are you people going to sit in the dark in an air-pocket, wanking each other off?

Morning Star, Friday 9 June 2000

Bailing out historical bilge

Andrew Murray, Eyes Left
Your ship has sunk, brothers! Thus did celebrity author Louis de Bernieres respond to criticism of his reactionary novel Captain Corelli's Mandolin in this space last year.

This column accused him of crude anti-communism and, in an unexpected reply, he accused the Morning Star of … well, we'll come to that.

Now it seems that de Berniere's own vessel is shipping water fast and the prospect of Hollywood dollars has finally persuaded him to try to bail out some of his bilge.

A year after pouring scorn on his political critics, he has admitted, in a limited sense, that he was wrong and that, actually, when it comes to the Greek politics that were central to Captain Corelli's Mandolin, he doesn't have a clue what he was talking about.

To recap, the novel in question is an apologia for the Greek right wing, including the dictator Metaxas.

It presents the Italian occupation of Greece as a bit of a laugh.

And, most strikingly of all, it depicts the communists who fought hardest, and often alone, against the fascists and the nazis, as brutes, rapists, ignorant demagogues and cowards.

It is a classic work of fin-de-siecle anti-communism.

In fact, it fits hand in glove with the whole campaign – which has academic, creative and narrowly political aspects – to present the great problem of the 20th century as being communism and communists, while those who fought against them deserve indulgent treatment, no matter what their excesses.

In a letter published in last Sunday's Observer newspaper, de Bernieres conceded that while "I haven't actually changed my mind … I might be wrong, " adding that the history of the Greek resistance to the occupation "is extremely complex" and that he had never meant his book "to stir up bad blood."

The immediate cause of this limited act of repentance appears to have been difficulties which arose in the making of the film of the book – a Hollywood blockbuster set, like the novel, on the Greek island of Cephalonia.

Local people, who are rather better informed about what happened in Greece during the war than de Bernieres, were concerned that the film could reopen old wounds by traducing their history and wanted reassurances from the film-makers.

In fact, de Bernieres is only bowing to the inevitable. His game was already up.

The first clue was that the Greek edition of his book had some of the most brazen anti-communist episodes removed or toned down.

Why, if the author believed them to be historically accurate, was this necessary?

The answer, of course, is that, in Greece, he could not make the same assumptions about the events described as he does elsewhere.

One person who knows him well, but opposes his views on Greece, told me that "he is a person who knows little about politics."

If true, it is worth inquiring as to where the politics in Captain Corelli's Mandolin come from.

An answer appears on the book's back page, where the author presents his acknowledgements.

He thanks Alexandros Rallis of the Greek embassy in London, among others.

Mr Rallis was indeed third secretary at the embassy at the time when de Bernieres was researching, if that is the word, the background to his novel.

But it may be more interesting to note that Mr Rallis is also the grandson of Ioannis Rallis, the collaborationist dictator of Greece during the nazi occupation who was vicious in his persecution of communists and, indeed, anyone opposing the nazis.

I do not know if the younger Mr Rallis shares his grandfather's views or admired his quisling conduct.

But I do know that, if you drew research on Spain exclusively from a descendant of Franco or on Italy from Mussolini's granddaughter, you would either have to declare the fact or risk the suspicion of purveying a politically tainted perspective.

At any event, de Bernieres has been conceding privately that he "got it wrong," perhaps because of the guidance of Mr Rallis, for some time.

Now Hollywood has made him backtrack publicly, leaving all concerned with the film able to emphasise that it is "just a love story."

Well, there's not much joy in heaven here over this quasi-repentant sinner.

His book, which is unchanged outside Greece, remains on display in every bookstore.

It remains a vile libel on those who fought against fascism in Greece and, by extension, the communist resistance to the nazis throughout Europe.

Thousands of Greek communists fought and died for the freedom of their country.

They were hunted down by Greek rightwingers as well as the nazis themselves, since the former vastly preferred rule by a German fascist to rule by a Greek leftwinger.

After the war, Greece became the only country in Europe in which having taken part in the great struggle against the nazis was regarded as a crime.

These are the facts. Perhaps de Bernieres knew as much when he wrote his original letter to this paper.

He did not seek to dispute a single point which I had raised, preferring instead vulgar anti-communist venom.

This is how the lion of literary London ended his letter: "How long are you people going to sit in the dark in an air pocket, wanking each other off?"

Well, maybe he was just starting his next novel, with one eye on selling the rights to the seedy side of the US film industry.

At any event, whatever we get up to at the Morning Star, it sure beats pimping for fascism.

Morning Star, Friday 15 September 2000

Retreat before reaction

Andrew Murray, Eyes Left

This week, Britain has been witnessing the first draft of a new reactionary mobilisation – a mustering and manipulation of those forces which represent a mortal danger to the labour movement and everything that it stands for.

As with the anti-paedophile hysteria whipped up by the Murdoch press this summer, a social crisis has been engineered by the sworn enemies of democracy and social justice.

And, yet again, new Labour's high command has been in disarray – weak, confused and on the run from events – at a moment when clear political leadership has never been more essential.

Two forces stand behind the fuel-tax protests which all but brought the country to a halt this week.

First, and most obviously, are the giant oil monopolies.

Their self-interest is clear – a cut in fuel-tax duties will lead to far more petrol being sold and the lower prices will not cause the slightest dent in the already vast profits of Shell, BP and Esso.

That is why the tankers were not stirring from their refineries.

In most cases, the "pickets" mounted by road hauliers and farmers hardly constituted a serious obstruction to the tankers leaving,

It was the bosses of the oil giants who were happy to see the political squeeze being put on the government.

If this has been a blockade, it has been a blockade by big business, with the farmers, cabbies and lorry owners but pawns in their game.

The second motivating force has been the Conservative Party, its supporters in the press and the flotsam and jetsam of reactionary groupings which regard even this pusillanimous Labour government as an affront to the natural order of things.

For these people, the hauliers are hailed as heroes, even as they engage in the sort of "holding the country to ransom" behaviour which would be damned as the ante-room to anarchy had it been

245

undertaken by the organised working class in any shape or form.

Those who rail against anyone who trespasses on the sanctity of the "rule of law" when that is identical with the rule of profit have indulged, with their blessing, a mobilisation against law and the community this week.

It is not hard to see why. The independent lorry owners, many of them battle-scarred veterans of strike-breaking anti-trade unionism, together with the manipulated anti-paedophile mobs and some of the forces grouped around the Countryside Alliance, represent a strike force for reactionary politics which sections of the ruling class seem increasingly ready to mobilise against democracy.

Democracy, alas, is under faltering leadership in Britain at present.

The thundering denunciations of lawbreakers and the patronising lectures on support for the rule of law which would have been forthcoming had this been trade unionists in action were all missing from ministers this week.

Never has new Labour's terror of big business, of the right-wing press and of the enraged middle classes been more clearly on display.

As with their silence in the face of Murdoch's incitement to vigilantism under the guise of "child protection," new Labour's leaders make the ministers of Weimar Germany appear models of resilience and determination.

The demands behind which the hauliers and their associates mobilised are, no matter how popular they may be, wrong.

While it is true that indirect taxation is necessarily regressive and that funding schools and hospitals out of the petrol pump is a questionable enterprise, it is not necessarily true that fuel taxes are too high.

From the point of view of society as a whole, curbs on car use – and lorry use for that matter – deliver real benefits for the environment and the community, the more so now that the government is at long last putting serious money into improving public transport.

Certainly, any question of cutting fuel duties should only be considered in the round, alongside all these other factors.

The demand for the industrialised – or, to not be too mealy-mouthed, the imperialist – powers to put pressure on OPEC to increase production and thereby cut the price of crude oil is misguided.

Again, without consideration of all the connections in the world economy and the manner in which they are manipulated to the profit of those big powers, this demand is simply a bully's order for the world's entire economic life to be reordered to suit the consumption patterns of a small section of humanity.

Under the anarchy of the global market, OPEC member states have the same right to secure the best price that they feel they can command for what is generally their only natural resource.

Coming from those states which have failed to do anything to reduce the crippling burden of debt on the world's poorest people, putting pressure on OPEC is rank hypocrisy.

No, any solution to the problem of energy prices must start by tackling the cause of the problem – monopoly control of every link in the chain, from raw material production to retailing.

If ever a group of companies had earned the right to be taken under public control on account of their anti-social behaviour, it is BP, Shell and Esso this week.

Indeed, only economic planning on the broadest scale, both nationally and internationally, can eliminate the root causes of the crisis.

For the labour movement, the priority must be to stand firm against this reactionary offensive.

But it still needs to go further and find the ways and means of winning those sections of the people currently being manipulated by the monopolies and their media into an alliance which addresses their concerns while directing their anger at the real enemy.

TUC general secretary John Monks used congress in Glasgow to give a welcome lead, correctly calling the unfolding crisis a "bosses' blockade."

Indeed, more or less the whole TUC responded in a clear class way, with the T&G in particular standing firm in its resistance to the "blockade."

Some of the language in the general council statement will come back to haunt it, however.

Talk of "holding the country to ransom" is the stock-in-trade of anti-union punditry and will no doubt be trotted out against organised labour the next time that it takes industrial action.

The truth of this week's events is that the ruling class is ready to "hold the country to ransom" every day of the week.

This was more than just the oil monopolies flexing their muscles, it was a dry run for counter-revolution.

Lest this sound unduly alarmist, look at the coverage in the Tory press.

The Daily Telegraph, using arguments which are a clear echo of Chilean reaction in 1973, justified the "civil disobedience" on the grounds that Britain was no longer a real parliamentary democracy, so insurrection by what it celebrated as the "forces of conservatism" was not only right but necessary.

Boris Johnson, who is shortly to become a Tory MP, noted gleefully that the police were clearly unwilling to mobilise against the protesters because they sympathised with them.

The Daily Mail, which has always urged that the full force of the state be deployed against the mildest expression of trade unionism, told the government that it must never use "British coppers against British truckers" – unless they are members of the T&G presumably.

Simon Heffer warned that middle-class "revolutionaries" may soon be more than a "figment of Arthur Scargill's imagination."

This is the authentic voice of bitter bourgeois violence, and all directed against this milk-and-water apology for a centre-left government!

Some trade unionists may indeed have hoped to see the forces of the state deployed against the protesters this week.

That is an illusion. Under these circumstances, if the state were to mobilise, it would be against democracy and Downing Street, not BP and the hauliers.

The labour movement must learn these lessons, and fast. Reaction is mobilising its forces for a sustained attack on democracy and labour.

The government is faltering in its resistance, because its craven support for big business and the tabloid agenda has prepared the way for this situation.

This week's lesson in the class struggle has been written in petrol. A policy retreat before reaction will lead to the next lesson being written in blood.

Veterans warn of 'new Hiroshima'

Brian Denny

Environmental campaigners and Gulf war veterans warned of a "new Hiroshima" yesterday due to contamination from depleted-uranium (DU) weapons used in the Balkans and Iraq.

British Gulf war veteran Ray Bristow said that over 40 British veterans had already been shown to have been contaminated following tests in Canada.

He said that there had been a massive increase in cases of leukaemia and cancer in Iraq, where DU weaponry was widely used.

"If you include the 5,000 Iraqi children dying every month, plus Iraqi and coalition casualties from such contamination, we are looking at a death rate on a scale of a new Hiroshima," said Mr Bristow.

"The use of these weapons, which are deemed illegal by the United Nations, is a crime against humanity and Western leaders who order their use are themselves war criminals," he said.

In a sign of world-wide concern, Portugal ordered medical tests for its soldiers serving in Kosovo to check for radiation from DU weaponry following a death of a soldier.

Portuguese Defence Minister Castro Caldas is following steps taken by his counterparts in Belgium and Spain.

The father of a Portuguese corporal who died after serving in Kosovo is demanding that his son's body be exhumed and tested for radiation.

"It was depleted uranium that killed him." said Luis Paulino, whose

---

The Morning Star was the first national daily newspaper in Britain to splash on the dangers of depleted uranium weaponry, a topic which became prominent in the press in the opening weeks of 2001.
Brian Denny is foreign editor of the Morning Star.

son Hugo died in March, three weeks after returning to Lisbon. He has called for a new autopsy because defence ministry officials have yet to explain the cause of his son's death.

A Ministry of Defence spokeswoman in Whitehall dismissed all evidence that DU weapons presented any sort of radioactive risk, saying: "There's more danger from radiation in a granite wall."

However, Campaign Against Depleted Uranium co-ordinator Rae Street said the casualties so far were the "tip of the iceberg.

"Our own government is not admitting that depleted uranium is dangerous and is committed to its use, but, if it has not been proved safe, it should not be used.

"There is a lot of evidence of its effects on Gulf war veterans and innocent people who are living in regions where it has been used," warned Ms Street.

Italy said that it did not know that DU arms had been used in Bosnia by NATO, just days after an inquiry was launched into why military personnel had been dying of leukaemia.

Defence Minister Sergio Mattarella affirmed that "10,800 DU projectiles had been fired by US aircraft," on Bosnia in 1994-5.

"I must express my bitterness that the competent international organisations have waited until now to answer our request for information which is important for the Bosnian community and members of the military," he said.

However, NATO claimed that DU rounds had been "fired from A-10 Thunderbolt aircraft, under international auspices," claiming that this had been known for years.

According to the independent Italian Observatory for the Protection of the Armed Forces, seven military personnel who served in the Balkans have died and 12 others are ill from exposure to radiation from DU weapons.

Also the Italian defence ministry confirmed that 11 personnel had recently developed leukaemia after taking part in Balkans "peace missions."

daily paper of the left

★ Morning Star

Incorporating the Daily Worker — for peace and socialism

Saturday January 1 2000   50p

A new battle to fight

BRITAIN'S labour movement faces sharp challenges in the new century, not least in rescuing the party that it established from being subverted from within by those who describe themselves as "New" Labour.

Many in the movement comfort themselves with the notion that the Labour Party has survived previous periods of domination by the party's right wing, but the New Labour faction is not simply a rehash of earlier expressions of right-wing social democracy.

Tony Blair and his acolytes make no secret of the fact that they despise the legacy of "Old Labour" in all its forms, socialist or social-democratic.

They reject traditional acceptance of the role of the state to promote economic planning, proclaiming their faith in market forces as the key regulator of economic activity.

They similarly reject the role of government to raise the living standards of the poor by means of nationalisation, public enterprise or progressive taxation.

Chancellor Gordon Brown's pro-business policies have included huge cuts in corporation tax and transferring the power to set interest rates to the unelected Bank of England.

He and the Prime Minister miss no opportunity to proclaim their desire to transform the Labour Party into the "party of business."

Mr Blair's hostility to the party that he is supposed to lead has descended to the level of publicly regretting its formation. He has expressed on several occasions his belief that the Lib-Lab coalition of the 19th century should not have been disturbed.

This view is in conflict with that of the overwhelming majority of party members and the broader labour movement, but clear indications of its intention to rebuild that coalition.

Apart from the government job offer to former Lib-Dem leader Paddy Ashdown, which was not reported to the Labour Party, the two men were glad to join Mr Ashdown's successor Charles Kennedy and former Tory Cabinet ministers Kenneth Clarke and Michael Heseltine in a Britain in Europe publicity stunt.

Mr Blair's readiness for a coalition of anti-Labour forces in opposition to the trade unions, to socialists and to all those loyal to Labour values is reminiscent of the betrayal by Ramsay MacDonald in the 1930s, with the so-called "National" government.

Turn to p2

Selected further reading

Almost any history of the 20th century would throw light on the times and endeavours of the Daily Worker and Morning Star, just as they shed ever fresh light on that history.

The books listed below are a selection of those works most relevant to this publication, either as the memoirs of members of the paper's staff and contributors or as histories of the paper, the left press or the Communist Party covering the period since the paper's foundation.

The wider history would, of course, require a much broader bibliography, but the books listed should provide readers with sufficient cross-reference to allow them to pursue their interests further.

About Turn: The British Communist Party and the Second World War: the Verbatim Record of the Central Committee Meetings of 25 September and 2-3 October 1939 edited by Francis King and George Matthews (London 1990)

A Man To Be Watched Carefully by Peter Zinkin (London 1983)

At The Barricades: Forty Years on the Cutting Edge of History by Wilfred Burchett (New York 1981)

A Weapon In The Struggle: The Cultural History of the Communist Party in Britain edited by Andy Croft (London 1998)

Breakfast With Mao by Alan Winnington (London 1986)

British Volunteers For Liberty: Spain 1936-1939 by Bill Alexander (London 1982)

Cockburn In Spain: Despatches from the Spanish Civil War edited by James Pettifer (London 1986)

Crossing The Line: Being the Second Volume of Autobiography by Claud Cockburn (London 1958)

For The Socialist Cause: the Class Struggle in the Times of My Forebears and Myself by Ernie Pountney (London 1973)

George Sinfield: His Pen a Sword: Memoirs and Articles collected by May Hill (London, no date)

History Of The Communist Party Of Great Britain: Volume Three by Noreen Branson (London 1985)

History Of The Communist Party in Britain 1941-1951 by Noreen Branson (London 1997)

Hungarian Tragedy by Peter Fryer (1956) (London 1997)

In Time Of Trouble: An Autobiography by Claud Cockburn (London 1956)

Opening The Books: Essays on the Social and Cultural History of British Communism edited by Geoff Andrews, Nina Fishman and Kevin Morgan (London 1995)

Our Flag Stays Red by Phil Piratin (1948) (London 1978)

Poor Men's Guardians: A Survey of the Struggles for a Democratic Newspaper Press 1963-1973 by Stanley Harrison (London 1974)

Science And Everyday Life by JBS Haldane (London 1939)

The Death Of Uncle Joe by Alison Macleod (London 1997)

The Greening Of A Red by Malcolm MacEwen (London 1991)

The Story Of The Daily Worker by William Rust (London 1949)

Tibet: Record of A Journey by Alan Winnington (London 1957)